THE STORY
of the
ORCHESTRA

By
PAUL BEKKER

W · W · NORTON & COMPANY
New York

COPYRIGHT, 1936, BY
W. W. NORTON & COMPANY, INC.
70 FIFTH AVENUE, NEW YORK

First Edition

PRINTED IN THE UNITED STATES OF AMERICA
FOR THE PUBLISHERS BY THE VAN REES PRESS

THE STORY OF THE ORCHESTRA

Books by Paul Bekker

THE STORY OF MUSIC

RICHARD WAGNER

THE CHANGING OPERA

THE STORY OF THE ORCHESTRA

Jan Breughel's "The Sense of Hearing"
Group of Instruments of the Seventeenth Century
(Madrid, Prado)

To
Mrs. M. D. Herter Norton

Contents

FOREWORD   xi

I. PRELUDE: *A Family Chronicle—The Instruments of the Orchestra*   15

II. THE CLASSIC ORCHESTRA OF *Haydn*   39

III. THE OPERA ORCHESTRA OF *Mozart*   68

IV. THE DYNAMIC ORCHESTRA OF *Beethoven*   88

V. THE ORCHESTRA OF ROMANTIC ILLUSION   118
   Weber
   Schubert
   Mendelssohn
   Schumann

VI. THE VIRTUOSO ORCHESTRA OF   142
   Berlioz
   Meyerbeer
   Liszt

CONTENTS

VII. THE COSMIC-ORCHESTRA OF *Wagner*   173

VIII. THE DECADENT ORCHESTRA OF   199
  Brahms
  Bruckner
  Mahler

IX. THE NATIONAL ORCHESTRA OF   228
  Verdi
  Bizet
  Smetana
  Tschaikovsky
  Sibelius

X. THE "ART-FOR-ART'S-SAKE" ORCHESTRA OF   256
  Strauss
  Debussy
  Puccini

XI. THE MECHANISTIC ORCHESTRA OF   284
  Schoenberg
  Stravinsky
  and the present time

INDEX   317

List of Illustrations

"The Sense of Hearing"	Frontispiece
Handel Festival in Westminster Abbey, 1784	31
Performance of Hadyn's "Creation"	43
Carl Maria von Weber	125
Berlioz and Liszt	163
Brahms	207
Tschaikovsky	251
Toscanini	291

Foreword

Brooding over a foreword for this book, I come to the conviction that there is nothing more superfluous than such forewords. Most of them show an annoying similarity with the introductory speeches of the clowns in *A Midsummer Night's Dream,* as, for instance, where Moonshine, disconcerted, sums up his prologue in the words: "all that I have to say, is, to tell you, that the lantern is the moon; I, the man in the moon; this thorn-bush, my thorn-bush; and this dog, my dog."

I plagiarize: all that I have to say is to tell you that this book is a book on the orchestra. I, the author of this book, these opinions my opinions———, and so on.

For what more?

Surely my well-meaning readers will see very soon that I intended to write neither a learned history of the orchestra, nor of the instruments—as Curt Sachs has done, to whom I am much obliged—nor a compendium of the orchestral forms, nor a dictionary

FOREWORD

of orchestral composers, nor, indeed, a systematic text-book. In spite of all such "neither-nors" I hope that this book may have to tell some things to those to whom all my books are addressed: the friends and lovers of music. If they should be interested in my discussion of how our modern orchestra came about I shall be satisfied. Everybody may take from it what he pleases and—perhaps—not be offended because I have written my book along the line of my own intentions and not of his.

All this seems to be self-evident and therefore superfluous to mention. But now I have to add a confession, namely: that this book is no translation. I wrote it from the beginning in English. I did so, indeed, not out of insolence. But after the field of German language had been closed to me, I felt the necessity to speak with my new friends as directly as possible—even if I should run the risk of losing some elegance and flexibility in the language. I think the author himself always will be better understood than the most dexterous translator, and the intellectual construction of the thoughts receives a more precise shape, even if the charm of the elocution should be diminished.

On the other hand, I am conscious of my venture. I never should have dared it, if some helpful friends had not assisted me. Among them I am obliged the most to Mrs. M. D. Herter Norton, without whose advice and active aid this book never would have been

FOREWORD

published. It is only a small tribute of gratitude if the dedication page bears her name.

A chronological table, as in *The Changing Opera,* seemed to be not suitable for this book, but all important dates are included in the index.

As for the rest, I refer again to my dear and honored model, Moonshine: "this English, my English, and these defects, my defects."

New York,   PAUL BEKKER.
September, 1936

I

Prelude: *A Family Chronicle*

The Instruments of the Orchestra

I

THE story of the orchestra resembles an old family chronicle, or, more exactly, the story of the rivalry among a large number of old families. Eventually they unite for a common aim and the establishment of regular affairs of state. The present-day orchestra seems to us to be quite a natural arrangement of the single parts and groups: the strings, the wood-winds, the brasses, the percussion. Nevertheless to choose these from an immense number of instruments, to put them in order, so that each should stand in its right place and accomplish the necessary functions, no more and no less—this was a task which claimed the work of about one and a half centuries. This work was done chiefly in the 17th century and the first half of the 18th, the orchestra in its present combination emerging about 1750.

Instruments have existed, of course, at all times and in great numbers, more in earlier days perhaps than there are today. Their purpose was to accompany the singing voices and also to substitute for such voices as were lacking. Furthermore, instruments were employed to play for dancing, for the marching of soldiers, and finally, in the church service. The wind instruments especially had an important ecclesiastical function, already in ancient times. We remember the "seven trumpets of rams' horns" of Jericho as well as the cymbals and harps of biblical songs of victory. We find these instruments in the old Babylonian and Egyptian sculptures. Also we learn that Greek virtuosi were required to perform upon their instruments for the Roman festivals.

From the beginning there have been several great types or families of instruments, classified according to method of sound-production. There were stringed instruments, there were the wind instruments, there were instruments of percussion. But none of the instruments common before 1600 still exists at the present time. Among our instruments, the violin type, an outgrowth of earlier stringed forms, was invented about 1600. Our wood-winds, such as the oboe and bassoon, are older, but their present shape dates from the 17th century. The clarinet was not invented until the 18th century. Even Haydn and Mozart did not use clarinets generally, because clarinet players were not always at hand. Horns and trumpets received their present forms during the 18th and 19th centuries. The flute and the percussion instru-

PRELUDE

ments have certainly existed since antiquity, but in very primitive forms.

Our instruments, as we know them, then, originated in the Renaissance and the subsequent periods. The tendency to combine them caused the construction of several types of the same instrument in different sizes. This was an imitation of the different ranges and qualities of the human voice. The violin, for instance, was constructed principally in three different sizes: a soprano type, called violin; an alto-type, called viola; a tenor and bass-type, called violoncello. The double-bass, which is still employed to-day in our orchestra, does not belong to the violin family. It is a survival of the gamba family, predecessors of the violins. The gambas had also existed in all registers. They had been, so to speak, the former royal family. But their tones had proved too soft to constitute a separate instrumental body. The subsequent type of the violin, more slender and therefore offering more possibilities for technical development, with a singing quality like the gambas but more penetrating and capable of carrying, superseded the gambas. Only the double-bass because of its soft deep tones held its ground as the foundation of the subsequent quartet of strings.

With the establishment of a usable chorus of strings the basis of the modern orchestra was discovered. This orchestra was primarily an imitation of the singing chorus, so that the single instruments had to correspond to the single voices in versatility as well as in range. They had to be able to convey harmony with all its changes in a song-like manner. It was the special work of the 17th century to develop the instrumental types suitable for this purpose. Of course there existed no clear idea of such an aim. Nobody said or thought: we must create an orchestra. Nor was there any special literature for the instruments. All high-class music was intended to be sung, the instruments being only substitutes to replace absent voices. But in time these substitutes gained independence with their growing capacity for singing expressiveness and versatility of technique.

2

THE perfecting of the violin itself is one of the most remarkable achievements of musical history. The tone of the violin is distinguished by its astonishing similarity to the singing and emotional qualities of the human voice. Not only the tone, but the mechanical organization of the violin also approaches absolute perfection. Its shape is an achievement of artistic beauty and simplicity. Its four strings are related on the principle of the fifth, the most important interval of the harmonic system. Its fingerboard makes possible the performance of an extraordinarily wide range of tones, especially in the high range regions, the more restricted number of low tones, conditioned by the lowest string, being compensated for by

PRELUDE

the other members of the violin family, other instruments constructed on the same principle, only larger in size. In this way the full chorus of the violin type, from violoncello to soprano violin, represents a sound-body which surpasses human voices in variety both of pitch and of possible combinations. The violin family differs from the voice family chiefly in not being linked with human language. But even this apparent lack proved with time to be an important advantage, as became evident the moment words were felt to be an obstruction to the unhindered development of the play of musical sounds.

The violin type was fixed during the 16th century, its first great makers being Gasparo da Salo and Andrea Amati, who lived at this time. It was perfected during the following century, when Antonio Stradivarius (1644-1737) constructed his unsurpassed instruments. Since that time it has remained unchanged and unchangeable, a miracle among human inventions, because improvement seemed to be neither possible, nor necessary, nor desirable. Thereafter all that happened was—with the exception of mechanical improvement in the bow during the 18th century—the gradual combining of the different members of the violin family into a homogeneous group or choir, the development of the technique and manner of playing and, by degrees, the supplementing of the violin tone in ensembles by that of wind instruments.

The most significant feature of the modern or-

THE STORY OF THE ORCHESTRA

chestra is this: that it is based upon the violin choir, which sprang up in imitation of the singing chorus. *The violin choir has been the kernel of orchestral music during all its subsequent stages.*

3

THE winds were introduced by degrees. First they appeared occasionally to enhance the effect of the strings; after a time they came to be used in contrast with them. But the perfecting of wind instruments was from the beginning more difficult than that of the strings, because of the lack of a common type. There were originally two distinctive groups, the wood-winds and the metal-winds, going to show that all wind instruments derive their character primarily from the material of which they are made. Their particular characteristics depend further upon the vibrations and overtones of this material, upon their shape, their construction, and the manner in which they are blown. All metal-winds have a metallic tone, the woods the softer tone of their particular substances. Therefore the use and technique of all winds are conditioned by the nature of their materials. Metallic tones assume a heavy and ponderous character, and are qualified mainly for the accentuation of rhythmic and dynamic effects, just as they were formerly used in march and cult music.

From the earliest times there have been two types of tone-production in wind instruments: by direct

PRELUDE

contact of the lips, and by means of a vibrating reed or other mouthpiece. In the former case the tones are clear and steady, in the latter, tremulous and cloudy. From these contrasting sounds the organ, most complicated of wind instruments, is built up, its wind being mechanically supplied by a bellows, however, which sets it in a class apart. The wind instruments which gradually came to be used in the orchestra fall into two classes, known to us to-day as the wood-winds and the brasses. The principle of construction of the brasses is simple: a metal tube is blown into by means of a mouthpiece. That of the wood-winds varies with the different types. The flute, which nowadays is no longer of wood but is for convenience always included in the term wood-winds, sounds only by direct contact of the instrument with the lips of the player. The oboe, and its relatives—oboe d'amore, oboe di caccia, English horn, and bassoon—sound by a reed, from which the tone receives a more vibrant and hence more singing quality. Finally the clarinet, the youngest of the wood-winds, invented only during the 18th century, sounds by means of a beak mouthpiece with a reed, whence the tone acquires a particularly soft character.

The development of the winds was complicated by the construction of keys, stops, and valves, mechanical devices for extending their technical versatility and improving the quality of their tone. The construction of wind instruments was always being improved upon, and never came to a standstill with a single perfected type as was the case with the violin. In contrast to that classic string-type, the winds were incessantly changing.

The impulse that stimulated the combining of the winds with the strings may be traced to the organ. The organ was the first instrument to employ not only the different tone-colors in its pipes, but also the principle of doubling important single tones, especially the octave and the fifth, according to their harmonic importance. With this principle, proclaimed in a scientific way by the German Michael Praetorius (1571-1621), the old principle of polyphony was put aside and the new harmonic principle of writing in chords came to the fore. The horizontal line of the single voice was no longer considered authoritative, but was replaced by the vertical chord. All musical media had to subordinate themselves to achieving the most perfect performance of this chord, which was represented primarily by the strings, its important tones being emphasized by the woods and accentuated by the brasses. The percussion gave the final stress. Percussion in general has no exact tones, with the exception of the kettledrums and the bells; and even these were employed chiefly as dynamic and rhythmic elements.

So the idea underlying the orchestra on the whole is the representation of harmony by the choir of strings colored by wood-winds and accentuated by

PRELUDE

brasses and percussion. On this principle the first orchestras were built up. What we call the development of the orchestra is, seen from the outside, only *the story of the mechanical perfection of the wind groups and their ever more subtle interweaving with the strings.*

4

THE strings, then, were appointed the governing patrician family. They ruled the orchestra by an oligarchic system based upon the laws of harmony. But the establishing of this string government needed some preparation. The method of organizing the string choir was discovered only with time. Meanwhile other instruments—the cembalo or harpsichord—constituted the first link between the different instrumental voices.

The harpsichord, a descendant of the lute, was, as its name implies, a stringed instrument. It had a special string for each tone, and the tones were made by pressing down keys, which by a mechanical arrangement plucked or struck these strings. In this way the harpsichord could produce a complete harmony at one time, while the violin and other bowed instruments could produce, aside from some modest double-stoppings, only one tone. Thus the harpsichord was, so to speak, the counterpart of the organ, with this distinction: that the organ was an assemblage of blowing voices, while the harpsichord consisted of string voices. But there was a fundamental difference also between the harpsichord and the other stringed instruments. The tones of the bowed instruments could be sustained as long as desired, whereas the tones of the harpsichord died away the moment they had been produced.

Because of this relationship and contrast the harpsichord became the natural foundation of the new union of string instruments, to a certain extent the back-bone of the growing orchestra. The harpsichord produced the full harmony, above which the melody of the violin could be displayed. The harpsichord retained this function until the middle voices of the other strings, such as the second violin and the viola, became more independent and versatile. Furthermore the harpsichord represented the bass-voice. This became with time its most important function, because the bass itself became by degrees the leading voice. With the change from the polyphonic style of counterpoint to the homophonic style of harmony the single voices lost their individualities. They became parts, radiations from the one keynote, which generally was the bass. The writing of music changed accordingly. Only the bass-line and the melody were written down, each bass tone being provided with a number which indicated the harmony to be played upon it.

This practice was called figured bass or thoroughbass. It came into use with the disappearance of the

PRELUDE

polyphonic style and the growth of the harmonic style during the 17th century. Such instruments as the organ and the harpsichord proved to be the natural tools for the practice of thorough-bass. They could represent the bass-voice as well as the middle voices, which had to be improvised. They could also be combined with other instruments which carried the melody founded upon this bass and these harmonic middle voices.

Looking back, then, at the growth of the idea of a modern orchestra, we see first a few instruments of which the violin is the most important, being primarily an imitation of the human voice, but of more extensive technique and larger range, and free from the restrictions of language. The organ and the harpsichord proved to be especially suitable for the representation of harmony because they could produce various tones simultaneously. When they were combined with the violin, performance of the complete range of melodic and harmonic forces was achieved. With time the organ took second place because of its wind-instrument character and its scarcity. The harpsichord was more usual, more easily found, than the organ, and better adapted for secular uses, its string character making it especially suitable for combination with the violin. Gradually the violin itself attracted other members of its family, both the number and the types of the different voices being augmented, pushing the harpsichord by degrees into a subordinate position, until the string group gained absolute predominance. Finally the harpsichord disappeared, for it had become superfluous.

The wind instruments were also gradually being drawn in. At first there were only a few of them, chiefly wood-winds, and even these were not yet ranged in any precise order. Sometimes flutes were used, sometimes oboes or bassoons, occasionally trumpets and horns. Each was employed either alone with the strings or in arbitrary combinations, the arrangements in most cases depending only upon what instruments happened to be available. Presently the winds also were grouped in a certain order: flutes, oboes, horns, bassoons, answering to the quartet of the strings. With time, when clarinets, trumpets, trombones were also employed, the whole wind section of the orchestra took on a certain similarity to the organ. The uniting of all these different instrumental types finally resulted in an organization of sounds, which, combining all the effects that had formerly been confined to the harpsichord and organ, offered not only a perfect representation of each voice, but also the greatest freedom of treatment and development.

5

THIS process of the organization of the orchestra covered a period of about 150 years, from about 1600 up to 1750, the so-called Late-Renaissance and Baroque era. This was a period of almost unlimited

PRELUDE

invention in all fields of musical activity: instruments, styles, forms. The monodic style superseded polyphonic music, the tendency towards harmonic simplicity and naturalness replaced what had become the artificiality of the contrapuntal style. Singing gained a new importance from the emphasis upon words, which had become incomprehensible in the old complicated forms.

As a result of these conditions opera came into existence in Florence about 1600. And with opera were connected the first experiments in the creation of an orchestra. But music unrelated to opera also turned in new directions. The activity of instruments, until then controlled by the laws of vocal form, received a special stimulus from the harmonic style. The introduction of equal temperament brought about increased use of major and minor instead of the former ecclesiastical modes. The 17th century especially shows a headlong superfluity, so to speak, of new media, new ideas, new tendencies, all urged on by the desire to create something absolutely new.

There are periods in human intellectual development when men live and think only in the past and take their rules of conduct from former times. The present, especially in music, is such an epoch. There are other periods in human history when men throw aside all memories of the past, because their creative impulse is so feverishly irresistible and overwhelming that everything they produce must be fresh and novel.

Such a period was this century and a half (1600-1750) in the field of music. There existed old instruments and new instruments, old styles and new styles, and men hardly knew how to employ this abundance of media. These men resembled children playing with a great many toys. The inventory of the Chapel of King Henry VIII of England mentions 64 string, 215 wind instruments. Queen Elizabeth maintained an orchestra of 40 musicians. The kings of France from the 16th century on retained two bands, the so-called *grande* and *petite écurie,* the latter, consisting chiefly of strings, for the aristocratic music of the court, the former consisting of oboes, trumpets, trombones, and drums, for the popular dances of the people. Also the Italian and even the German princes had their special orchestras, and the nobility in all countries followed this example, keeping the musicians at the same time as servants.

The chief instruments in former times had been lutes, theorbos, rebecs, violas, flutes, cornemuses, virginals, trumpets, trombones, drums. The lute family in particular kept its authoritative position for a long time, changing only by degrees, as we have seen, with the growing influence of the violin family, to the modern orchestral instruments and combinations. Monteverdi (1567-1643) in his Madrigal-book "Concerto," published in 1619 and dedicated to Catherine de Medici, calls for three choirs of instruments: the first consists of two bass lutes and cembalo

PRELUDE

and serves as accompaniment to the singing voice; the second includes the high strings and the completing continuo (violas, violins, and one cembalo); the third consists of the low strings (gambas or violoncello, double-basses and organ)—altogether 22 musicians. But the instrumental cast changed incessantly and some curious specimens were mixed in on occasion, such as giant double basses, windmills strung with ropes, cannons and bombs. Such things survive in Beethoven's "Battle of Vittoria."

But even in the 18th century, when a certain standard had been reached, the make-up of the orchestra was irregular and sometimes odd. The famous orchestra of the opera in Dresden, one of the most important orchestras of the Germany of that time, consisted, about 1750, of eight first and seven second violins, four violas, three violoncellos and three double-basses, approximately a normal string cast. In addition there were 2 flutes, 5 oboes, 5 bassoons, 2 horns, trumpets, and kettledrums. Very astonishing is the relatively large number of oboes and bassoons, but this is a characteristic feature of this period. We learn that on the occasion of a Handel festival in Westminster Abbey in 1784 the orchestra contained 6 flutes, 26 oboes, 26 bassoons. The strings were also represented in large numbers, to be sure, with forty-eight first, forty-seven second violins, twenty-six violas, twenty-one violoncellos, fifteen double-basses; and there were, besides, twelve trumpets, twelve horns, and six trombones. Nevertheless the number of oboes and bassoons seems to be disproportionately high.

Such careless experimentation with an abundance of media, used not because of organic necessity but only because of their fortuitous existence, illustrates the spirit of the Baroque period: its consciousness of power, its tendency toward extravagance and splendor, its obsession with innovations. The instruments existed, and because of their existence they had to be employed, no matter what the mixture. Their chief task was still to accompany the voice, but increasing liberties were allowed. Monteverdi's first books of madrigals, apparently written for an a-cappella choir only, must be regarded as to be performed with improvised instrumental ornamentation. The composer Graziani, living at the end of the 17th century, left the accompaniment to his voice parts entirely to the improvisation of the players.

Some of the new orchestras, on the other hand, grew up through imitation of the organ. This is true of Bach's orchestra. He did not write real orchestra compositions in the modern sense. His Brandenburg Concertos represent a chamber-music type and their cast is exceedingly varied, with no clear principle of orchestral organization. Handel's Concerti Grossi and some of his other occasional instrumental compositions are constructed along the lines of the Concerto of that time, alternating between a small and a large

*Handel Festival
in Westminster Abbey
1784*

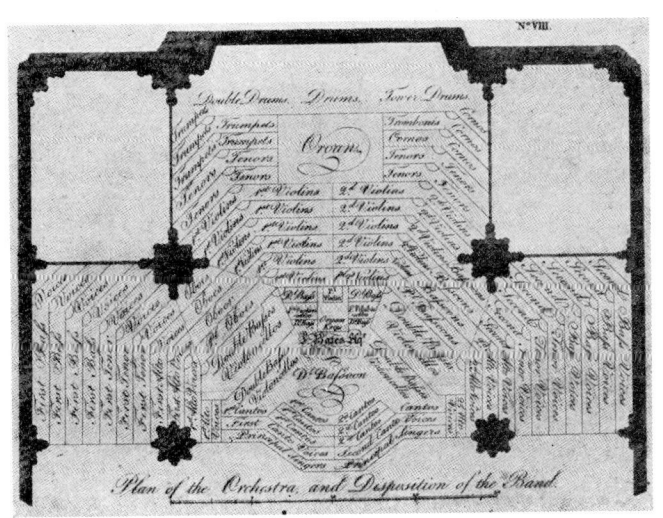

group of strings, with some winds. But in all these works and even more in the accompaniment of Handel's Oratorios and Bach's Cantatas and Passions, we perceive the perhaps unconscious imitation of the organ. The orchestral voices, especially the horns, trumpets, oboes, and other winds, must be viewed as complementary to the organ which still rules the tonal thought of these masters.

An important stimulus for orchestral music came about with the *collegia musica*. These gatherings united, particularly in Germany and Switzerland, all persons interested in music, at first the university people, subsequently the citizens' families. These collegia musica came into existence about 1700 in all university cities. In time they became the starting points for the later municipal concerts, such as the Gewandhaus concerts in Leipzig. In London some enterprising men—Banister, Britton and King—had arranged public musical entertainments in the last quarter of the 17th century. In Paris the composer Philidor organized the famous "concerts spirituels" in 1725. They represented the first public musical entertainment in France outside the church. The types of instrumental forms, called Suites or Partitas, of which the music made use, were taken chiefly from the dance. But this dance was no longer executed in reality, it was, so to speak, danced only in fancy, thus becoming idealized and serving as the basis of a new intellectual entertainment.

The church also had organized public concerts, detached from worship. The most famous of these concerts were given during the 16th and 17th centuries in Venice by Andrea and Giovanni Gabrieli and in Rome by Frescobaldi. These church concerts continued as long as the church continued to attract a sufficient number of people. But in the same measure as the church lost its general importance, secular musical entertainment gained ground. There were in England the great choral concerts for the performance of Handel's oratorios, a kind of religious opera represented off the stage. There were in Germany the societies, where citizens and students played for their own amusement and that of their families. There were the aristocratic circles of great princes, who kept their special orchestras, made up of the servants, conducted by a composer who was obliged to write such music as the count, or the prince, or the archbishop wanted. This spreading of music advanced the cultivation of instrumental and orchestral art and awakened and encouraged musical talent in general. There were, finally, by about the second third of the 18th century, the traveling virtuosos, especially of the violin, the harpsichord, and the organ, who, to display their abilities, arranged private and public meetings, that is to say, instrumental concerts.

PRELUDE

6

ALL these conditions go to show that these instrumental activities themselves—whether on a single instrument or on several, whether for worldly or ecclesiastical entertainment, whether in public or in private—were much more important than the music they brought forth. The fact of the playing, of making sounds, the naïve and primitive enjoyment offered by the performance itself, attracted the greater interest. The critical appreciation of the music performed, interest in musical forms as intellectual creations, was secondary. Of course the creative musician had to invent his own melodies, but nobody was offended if another composer's ideas were incorporated.

During its first period especially orchestral music had to lean for inspiration upon earlier vocal works. There were at first no distinctions between vocal and instrumental literature, nor any special indications for instruments in the notation of the music. Only the notes were given, and they were to be performed as well as possible, either by voices or by instruments. But new instrumental effects came into being and from these effects grew up new forms. Because of these new effects and these new forms exactness in notation became necessary. The first and basic new effect discovered was the possibility of *dynamic antithesis*. It was first employed by the Gabrielis in Venice and originated probably from the contrasts of two instrumental choirs, posted in the two opposite galleries of the Cathedral of St. Mark. This dynamic antithesis, an offshoot of the echo effect, could be produced by the contrast between a small and a large group of instruments—the principle of the concerto grosso. The same antithesis could be produced by a single group, playing alternately forte and piano. This was already an indication of a later stage, because it supposed a more highly cultivated ensemble playing. In both cases the most important thing was not the quality of the musical idea, but the achievement of dynamic contrasts. Only with time, after this effect had become more usual, was the quality of the musical idea itself regarded with growing attention.

The second new effect was *instrumental coloring*. This was produced by varying the instrumental combinations and by employing the instruments themselves for solo and virtuoso purposes. From this idea sprang up the concerti grossi and sonatas da camera and da chiesa for one, two, or three violins, such as Corelli (1653-1713), and afterwards Vivaldi (1680-1743) wrote. Bach was the first to apply this idea to the piano and to write piano concertos. His Brandenburg Concertos likewise belong to this group of compositions, built upon the use of a changing orchestral cast and the consequently changing instrumental effects.

The third and most important new effect developed

PRELUDE

with time from the two preceding effects. From contrasting dynamics and contrasting instrumental colors arose the idea of a sharper thematic individualization. Originally the instrument had imitated the singing voice, by degrees it had discovered its own dynamic and coloristic effects. Now a new type of instrumental language seemed to be necessary, a type such as the harmonic style demanded: melodic material, that should be not only singing but flexible and malleable, suitable for carrying out all the possibilities introduced by the growth of the instruments.

This third new effect, then, found expression in the *thematic* development. Starting with simple instrumental figurations with their dynamic and coloristic contrasts, the themes gained by degrees substance and plastic individuality. They attracted and absorbed the types of vocal and terpsichorean expression, transformed them into different melodic forms, which were contrasted one with the other. In this way a new species of imaginary action grew up. Its performers were not visible and the idea of the play could not be reproduced by words. It was of a purely musical nature, performed only by sounds, and it took shape by utilizing the natural acoustic relations of these sounds. It was a play of the power of imagination alone. It expanded on a plane outside reality, and thereby stimulated the fancy, which required a new field of activity. The form which summarized and symbolized all these efforts, tendencies, and ideals, was the sonata.

With the arrival of the sonata, the story of the orchestra ceases to be a family chronicle. Henceforth it is no longer the story of families, of historically interesting events and certain important individualities. These families have now united for the fulfillment of the state's ideal: the modern orchestra. Having served in diverse forms and disguises and traveled various roads, this orchestra has now discovered its own new destination. Like a young adventurer who must try his hand at lowly work until he finds his true vocation, it has wandered over the whole world, through Italy, France, Germany, England. It has assisted dancing, singing, church-services, has everywhere received new stimuli. Now it has found the new formula which is to grant it independence.

This formula is a hitherto unknown medium of musical thought and construction. It is suitable for no vehicle of expression other than the instrument and especially the orchestra, the summation of all instruments. At last this orchestra is ripe for taking and holding its own place, no longer as a servant and for some other purpose, but for itself alone. In its own image it enters the world. And the musical form in which it achieves success and conquers the whole realm of music—with the exception only of opera—is the sonata form, called, when applied to the orchestra, the symphony.

II

The Classic Orchestra of *Haydn*

I

The appearance of the instrumental symphony marks the beginning of the real career of the orchestra in its present-day significance. The first great master whose creative work opened this new road was *Joseph Haydn*.

Haydn was born in 1732, the descendant of a family of Croatian wheelwrights in a village on the Hungarian border. His birth preceded by 24 years the birth of Mozart, whom he survived by 18 years. In the later part of his life, he became Beethoven's teacher. At the time of Haydn's birth, Bach, Handel and Rameau, not yet in their fifties, were at the zenith of their creative activity; Gluck was only 18 years old. At the time of Haydn's death in 1809 Beethoven was nearly 40 and had already done a large part of his life-work.

Thus Haydn represents the direct link between the 18th and 19th centuries, the centre of the so-called classic period of music. He belonged to the same generation as the poets Gellert (born in 1715), Lessing (1709), Herder (1744), the philosophers Rousseau (1712), Hume (1711) and Kant (1724). This means, that he belonged to that generation which taught the doctrine of enlightenment by reason. Haydn himself was neither a poet nor a philosopher, he never wrote anything but his music. But this music is founded upon the same intellectual assumptions as the work of his poetical and philosophical contemporaries, it breathes the same spirit. It was because of these conditions, that Haydn became the founder and first universal master, the patriarch, of modern orchestral music.

There has been and still is a tendency to belittle Haydn's importance with respect not to his musical genius but to his historical significance. Certainly there were noteworthy composers before him, who prepared the way for his work in developing the sonata form as well as the efficiency of the orchestra. Certainly there came after him Beethoven, who gave these forms a greater breadth and increased the efficiency of the orchestra far above the limits Haydn kept to. There is no need to underrate the works of the great successor or the merits of the less important predecessors. But neither can diminish Haydn's fundamental importance of work. That work is perfect in itself. It acquires many a stimulus from older masters, but it absorbs and brings these to fruition in an absolutely independent manner. It runs its course to its own fulfillment, needing no later completion.

THE CLASSIC ORCHESTRA

All that came after Haydn started from new tendencies; nothing that preceded had yet reached the point from which Haydn started. He is an individuality closed within itself, directed by its own rules, striving after its unique aims. After the period of the orchestral family chronicle he is the first absolute monarch to rule over the realm of instrumental music. Conquerors and inventors preceded him and other kings succeeded him; but none of these can lessen the importance of his fundamental activity.

Haydn was a self-taught man. Of course, as a choir-boy at St. Stephen in Vienna, he received some instruction, but this instruction was without system and had nothing to do with his reaching the ultimate goal. His work was based chiefly on incentives either fortuitous or instinctive. Phenomena like Bach or Handel grew up as recipients of a traditional style of composition and of instrumental culture, centering about the organ. Haydn had nothing like this to guide him. He played violin and piano, but he had to study even these instruments without a really authoritative teacher, depending chiefly upon his hearing and capacity for imitation. The compositions he heard and sang as a choir-boy were in the main contemporary Italian productions of no deep-rooted importance. When he left St. Stephen at the age of 18 because of the breaking of his voice, he had to look after himself in both economic and artistic matters. He continued to learn the prevalent method of singing with the famous singing-teacher Porpora, whose pupils he accompanied. At the same time he continued the study of instrumental composition, especially through the works of Philip Emanuel Bach, which caused a certain sensation at the time because of their wealth of feeling, expressed by the new harmonic style.

However, there was neither a system nor a clear plan in all these occupations. Haydn took what he found. He lived from hand to mouth, from one moment to the next, in his artistic and economic existence. His chief desire was to continue his own composition. He wrote sonatas for the piano, pieces for the voice, even an opera which was commissioned. In this way his talent gradually became known and noticed. In 1755 he was invited to a musical circle in the country at Weinzierl, near Melk in Austria. Here there was a small orchestra, consisting of some strings and a few winds. For them Haydn composed his first quartets, a symphony and also divertimenti, notturnos, cassationes for orchestra. Weinzierl was only a summer residence, and Haydn returned to Vienna to give lessons; but after some time he was given an engagement as conductor-composer to the Count Morzin in Lucavec (Bohemia). When Morzin died, Prince Esterhazy summoned Haydn for his orchestra, which was maintained first in Eisenstadt and afterwards in his newly-built country residence of Esterhaz.

Performance of Haydn's "Creation"

With this appointment Haydn had reached his goal. He remained with Prince Esterhazy most of his remaining life, from 1761 until 1790. The independence of his development was thus preserved, for at Esterhaz Haydn lived apart from the world, relying only on his own interior resources. Of course many visitors came there, among them famous virtuosos of that time; and also the Prince moved the orchestra with his complete household to Vienna during the winter. Consequently Haydn knew all the important musicians of his time, especially Mozart, who gained his admiration and love. Apart from these trips he became acquainted with all noteworthy musical productions that interested him. Despite primitive postal service and the absence of publicity, people of this period were quite as well informed as we are about remarkable events and contemporary productions. The musicians especially were acquainted with everything that happened in their field and this almost as soon as it happened, despite the lack of publishers, newspapers, and railways. Bach in Leipzig knew well the compositions of the famous Italian and French musicians of his time. Likewise Haydn in Eisenstadt could survey the instrumental productions of his contemporaries. If he did not make much use of them, it was only because he did not need them. He went on his way, and this way had quickly led him to the top of the new instrumental art.

His fame spread to all musical circles, not only

in Austria and in Germany, but also in France and in England. Already in 1781 he received an invitation from Le Gros, director of the concerts spirituels in Paris. Many of his works were published in France. England likewise was very early interested in Haydn and in 1787 he was invited to visit London; but it was only after the death of Prince Esterhazy that he could be induced to undertake such a long trip. This was in 1790. Then he went to England twice in three years, proclaimed by the whole world as the first master of music. In London he crowned his life's work: he wrote his famous last twelve symphonies. Then, after his return from the second journey, stimulated by the Handel oratories he had heard, he composed his two great secular hymns to nature: "The Creation" and "The Seasons." This last work, which ended Haydn's activity, was finished at about the same time that Beethoven wrote his Second symphony.

2

The course of Haydn's life illustrates the development of his creative work. He never went to Italy, though this was then the usual source of education for the German composer. Gluck advised him to do so and apparently only the opportunity was lacking. Haydn himself however did not care much about such an opportunity. Perhaps he asked himself—consciously or not—what he should do and learn in

Italy? He may have felt that he had to follow paths different from those of the composers of opera, though he may not have realized that his task lay in the discovery of quite a new field of musical activity. Probably only his instinct kept him from making a superfluous trip to Italy, which would only have disturbed him and diverted him from his main purpose. At any rate, Haydn did not receive his higher education from study in Italy, because in truth Italy could not give him what he wanted.

Nor, for the same reason, did he find the right teacher. Not because of his poverty or the necessity of working steadily to make money. But who could teach him things which did not yet exist? Haydn had to grow up self-taught for the simple reason that no one was capable of instructing him in unknown matters. His seclusion in Eisenstadt and Esterhaz until his 60th year enabled him quite naturally to do his work in accordance with only his own intentions. He was like the inventor whose experiments succeed the better the less they are disturbed.

A striking similarity is evident here between Bach's and Haydn's lives. Bach also did not go to Italy because of the lack of opportunity. Bach also lived and created his works within a small circle of musical activity, in Arnstadt, Mühlhausen, Coethen, Weimar, and, chiefly, Leipzig. Bach also could do and write as he liked. Both Bach and Haydn had to observe only one fundamental condition: that their works be suitable for immediate practical purposes. They were not written with any speculative or ideal aim, nor with intent to publish or to make a world-wide effect. They were written only for *practical* use, for performance within the next week or for the next great holiday. All further results were accidental and in no way the product of the original creative intention.

Thus the only conditions governing Haydn's composition were laid down by exterior circumstances. His individual productiveness manifested itself in the fructifying of these circumstances, developing new inventions from them. This work was supported by the general demand for a new instrumental art. In Weinzierl he found a so-called country-house-orchestra of strings, 2 oboes, 2 horns. In Lucavec Count Morzin disposed of 12 to 16 musicians, among them an English horn and a bassoon player. The orchestra in Eisenstadt was somewhat larger. There were 5 violins, 4 violoncellos, 1 flute, 2 clarinets (for 2 years only), 4 oboes, 2 bassoons, 6 horns, and a harp. Trumpets and kettledrums were also available from the military band. Most of the musicians had to perform some domestic service, but the positions were much sought after. Esterhazy paid the best salaries and the reputation of his orchestra quickly increased with Haydn's growing fame. It included some outstanding musicians, notably the violinist Tommasini, reputed to be an eminent master of his instrument.

THE CLASSIC ORCHESTRA

Since a chorus was needed for the church service and the opera, the writing of music of these types was included in Haydn's obligations; but though Haydn wrote a number of masses and operas, he himself did not esteem them too highly, especially the operas. When they were wanted for performances at other places he declined with the argument that they had been written with regard only to the particular conditions existing in Eisenstadt. As for the ecclesiastical compositions, they show his handwriting but little of his genius. In vocal music this genius could unfold only when based upon a highly organized orchestra, and this combination Haydn mastered only after the composition of the London symphonies, in the two great oratories, "The Creation" and "The Seasons." These are no longer primarily vocal works, as are Handel's oratorios. They are orchestral works, completed and enhanced by the chorus and solo voices. The London symphonies, written for an orchestra of about 40 musicians with all the instruments available at that time for symphonic music, remain the acme of Haydn's work.

Thus Haydn's creative activity was founded chiefly upon instrumental compositions. This was the realm he was destined to discover, conquer, and cultivate. His development proves that he himself perceived this particular task with increasing clearness. Haydn began with piano music, in accord with his needs as a teacher, and he continued this line occasionally in later years, but not with any special interest, not with the sense of permanent importance which Beethoven always attached to piano music. Haydn next devoted himself to chamber music, stimulated by his employment in Weinzierl, Lucavec, Eisenstadt. There was at first no difference in principle between his chamber and his orchestral music; his so-called first quartet may as well have been his first symphony, written in Weinzierl. But with time Haydn separated these two types. As soon as he had discovered the string quartet as the four-voiced representative of harmony, he kept this type as the fundamental form, to some extent surpassing even the orchestra in importance.

In certain respects the string quartet represents in fact a tonal organism of absolute perfection. Because of the homogeneity of its sound colors it affects the hearer like a single instrument played by four players. It is, so to speak, a violin with the harmonic manifoldness of the piano. It is superior to the keyboard instrument in the singing character, the malleability, the unlimited possibilities for duration of its tones. It embodies in an absolute union both the independence and the intimate interrelationship of the voices. It is one and four at the same time. Thus the string quartet is the medium for an ideal transubstantiation of the polyphonic style into the new harmonic order.

In Haydn's treatment the first violin was the uncontested leader of this union. The main function of the three other voices was to accompany the soprano. This melodic-harmonic setting was the result of Haydn's tendency toward freedom from the bonds of the harpsichord's thorough-bass. His string quartet represented an independent type of instrumental music without the continuo. This independent organization of four voices made possible the use and display of thematic development because of the mobility and the similarity, sometimes close even to the point of identity, of the sounds.

3

HAYDN had discovered the models and principles for this thematic development in the works—more particularly the piano works—of *Philip Emanuel Bach* (1714-1788). Philip Emanuel, the second son of Johann Sebastian, was in Haydn's time more famous than his father. Even Mozart said about him: "he is the father and we are the boys." He had been educated in the rigid contrapuntal style of the older generation. But stimulated by his virtuosity as a piano player and by the discovery of new potentialities in the harmonic style, he soon threw away the traditional polyphonic media or subordinated them to the dominant idea of harmonic development. Subjects were changed to themes. The outlines of these themes were made to accord with the character and the technical qualities of the instrument. The form of their development was no longer directed by the rules of counterpoint, but became a free arrangement, following only a certain order of harmonic construction. The building up of this harmonic organism was the chief aim; the course of the single voices, their participation in what had formerly served as the development of the subject, now became only a medium for the evolution of harmonic expression.

Philip Emanuel had not only established the principle of thematic development and of melodic display over the basic harmony. Carrying on the models of his father and certain famous French and Italian masters, such as Domenico Scarlatti, Pergolese, Durante, Tartini, Gaviniés, he had established the form of the piano sonata. The sonata movement was at first an instrumental movement expanding on a single phrase, subjected as time went on to more varied development. Afterwards a second theme was added in order to provide some change of harmony. This second theme had its own individuality, being chosen to contrast with the first theme both in key and in melodic character. If, for example, the first theme was vivacious in character, the second would be of a more lyric type. From such contrasts the sonata movement acquired the character of a dialogue between opposite types of expression. This was a way of compensating the hearers for the lack of explanatory words, and this art of instrumental music opened up fields of activity hitherto unknown.

But thematic development was only one manifestation of the new style. From the harmonic relations between bass and soprano there had sprung up a new type of singing treble, called *melody*. To a certain extent it represented radiations of the bass in a well arranged order so that the bass and the treble always complemented one another, the two together embodying the productive harmonic impulse. This singing melody required a special position in a movement of distinctly lyric character; hence the second movement of the sonata.

The construction of this slow movement, based upon the song form, also followed the principle of thematic development. But the unfolding of the melody remained the organic purpose and the significant feature of this movement. As a slow melodious movement did not provide a good finish to the form, another lively movement, but of less importance than the first, was added to these two.

The process by which that instrumental form called the sonata came into being embraced a period of more than fifty years and was affected by many influences from other instrumental forms. Primarily by the suite, a series of dance pieces, differently arranged in different countries: in Germany, Italy, France. Also by the overture. The name "sonata" originally meant piece to be sounded (played) in contrast with the "cantata" or piece to be sung. All these names: sonata, overture, suite, changed frequently in meaning and there exists no exact classification. The Italian overture, established by Alessandro Scarlatti (1659-1725), consisted of the three types of movement: fast, slow, fast. The French overture, established by Lully (1632-1682), showed just the reverse: slow, fast, slow. This second type with time became restricted to opera. From the Italian type sprang the concerto, consisting of three separated movements. From the first of these the sonata movement gradually developed and in time the name sonata came to be applied to the whole form.

This evolution was brought to a certain stage of completion by Philip Emanuel. With his clavier-sonatas he fixed the general form of the sonata as a whole: the opening sonata movement, developed thematically; the melodious, slow second movement, a song type; the finale in the nature of a light dance or rondo (a "round song" with steadily recurring theme). Haydn took over Philip Emanuel's principles of form, and now added, perhaps to some extent influenced by the Mannheim composers, a fourth movement to the established three. This was the minuet, and it was inserted between the second and third movements. The minuet was the most characteristic dance of that time, popular in all social circles, and had naturally taken its place in the instrumental suite of the period. Because of its well accentuated three-beat rhythm it provided an intermediate type between the slow movement and the fast finale of the sonata.

4

PHILIP EMANUEL's instrument was the piano. He also wrote symphonies, but only upon occasion. At the piano he felt himself free and forceful; it was the instrument most accessible to him, both handed down by tradition and in the practice of his profession as a teacher and as accompanist to Frederick the Great of Prussia.

For Haydn the piano was only a halfway station on the road to the *string quartet*. This latter seemed to him an incomparably richer and more productive instrument, less bound by material restrictions. Haydn's creative work is on the whole, therefore, based upon the quartet, which also furnished the groundplan for his orchestral works. But there was a striking difference between the qualities of the quartet as a chamber and as an orchestral organization. The chamber-music quartet gave the single instruments much more freedom because they were played by soloists. The first violin and the cello especially could be treated in virtuoso style. In the orchestral quartet, however, several players had to perform the same parts, which meant that the demands made upon the performers underwent certain reductions. But the orchestral quartet compensated for this loss by the gradual addition of wind instruments which made possible many new effects.

Both the increased number of instruments playing

the same voice and the joining to them of winds were dynamic effects, causing a change in the strength of the tone. The sound could now be greatly increased or diminished by augmenting or reducing the number of instruments playing a phrase. This effect was not absolutely unknown. The old vocal music had already used the contrasts of forte and piano, especially for echo effects. The effectiveness of gradual transitions between piano and forte may also have been known. The single instrument, the solo violin especially, employed both direct contrasts of forte and piano and the crescendo and decrescendo or diminuendo. As soon as several instruments played one passage together, however, these effects were considerably increased.

This augmentation of the violins or combining of the winds with them may have been caused by the growing demand for such dynamic effects. As long as the voice had been dominant the use of dynamics was modest and occasional. But the more the special nature of the instrument came to be appreciated the more the development of dynamics was seen as a new musical resource. With this evolution of dynamics, the expression of an intensity of excitement, unattainable by the earlier vocal art, was disclosed as a possibility.

This growing dynamic impulse caused the gradual change from chamber music to orchestral music. The principle of augmentation brought consequences of unforeseen reach. With Haydn these remained from the first confined by certain definite conditions. His work being unalterably based upon the string quartet as the essence of the orchestra, his orchestral quartet was limited to a modest number of players, and the wind instruments simply followed the lines laid down by the strings. This meant that the limits of Haydn's orchestral dynamics were set by the dynamic limits of a small string choir.

If his work in the sonata form was related to Philip Emanuel Bach's constructive principles, Haydn's development of the orchestra was not unrelated to the work of certain predecessors. But there is one striking difference in the two relationships. While Haydn himself always acknowledged Philip Emanuel as his master—though he never saw him—he never mentioned his debt to his so-called precursors in the treatment of the orchestra. Apparently he himself did not estimate this influence very highly, otherwise he would not have left it unacknowledged. Yet it is not to be denied that especially the masters of the school of Mannheim, such as Stamitz, Cannabich, Richter, had brought the orchestra immediately before the time of Haydn's activity to an eminent virtuosity. The insertion of a second theme in the first movement, the abandonment of contrapuntal elaboration and of the thorough-bass cembalo, the utilization of thematic development, finally the adoption of the minuet into the symphonic form—all these symptoms of the new style were already present in the works of the composers of Mannheim. This city was at the time a musical centre because of its geographic and political position halfway between Germany and France. It was from Mannheim that Franz Gossec (1734-1829), born in Southern Germany, went to Paris and there became one of the most influential conductors. The compositions of the masters of the Mannheim school were known and played everywhere and were reputed to be authoritative models of orchestral writing.

There can be no doubt that Haydn knew the works of the Mannheim circle. Since he never mentioned them, however, we must believe that he found his own way in the main without their help. Why could not this have been possible? It is a foolish theory which maintains that whenever two events happen simultaneously or nearly so, the one must be influenced by the other. Just as frequently the same mechanical invention is made in two different places at one time, so innovations in the field of art may be tried simultaneously by several individuals independently of one another. The significance of the innovation lies with the individual who has the capacity to develop and utilize it. Seen thus, the Mannheim composers were figures of a day. Their works were forgotten within a short time and have now only historical interest. Haydn, on the contrary, and whether influenced by suggestions from their activity or not, concentrated and developed all the new tendencies in creative work of monumental importance and permanent value.

The form which Haydn cultivated in his orchestral works came to be called the *symphony*. He himself frequently employed the title *overture*. Like the terms concerto, suite, sonata, the name symphony has a complicated early history. It was first used in antiquity as a designation for parts sounding together. Later it marked a composition in contrapuntal style with accentuated harmonic effects. In this form it was applied to the first movement of the so-called German dance-suite. Finally it became the name for the sonata written for orchestra. Thus the term symphony took on its meaning accidentally and only with time developed its present significance. This was fixed by Philip Emanuel, the symphonists of Mannheim, and, finally, Haydn. The decisive factor in settling the definition was not the meaning of the term, but *the transference of the constructive principles of the piano and quartet sonata to the orchestra, organized as a quartet choir, its dynamic effects completed by the gradual addition of winds.*

5

HAYDN wrote in all 104 symphonies, a number which surpasses even that of his quartets. He left also a numerous group of so-called divertimentos, notturnos, cassationes, some of which were afterwards used as quartets. These compositions were built up first in five movements, with two minuets. Later Haydn restricted the movements to four: the opening allegro, sometimes beginning with a slow introduction, the adagio or andante, a song or variation form, the minuet, and the finale, in general a rondo-type. The instrumental setting depended on the instruments available. But the astonishing fact must be acknowledged, that Haydn did not always make use of the instruments at hand. He preferred to select and to change the cast. Present in every case is the string quartet, or, when the double-bass is included, the string quintet. Sometimes it is divided into a solo and a tutti group, an arrangement reminiscent of the earlier concerto grosso.

This string foundation is completed by winds in various ways. In his earlier symphonies, up to the Eisenstadt works, Haydn employs chiefly 2 oboes and 2 horns. It is very interesting to observe the various ways in which these instruments are used to round out the harmony, to accentuate important tones or even melodic phrases, so that in spite of their apparently subordinate functions they always present a characteristic picture. But this arrangement with 2 oboes and 2 horns was no general scheme. Haydn liked to experiment; almost every one of his works shows an individual sound organization. There is for instance an adagio for strings and 2 flutes; there is one symphony of 1766, in which the melody is car-

THE CLASSIC ORCHESTRA

ried by the combined tones of the violin and the cello—quite a new effect. There is a symphony, whose Finale is a set of variations in which oboe, flute, horn, alternate in performing the melody. There are symphonies containing bassoon, horn, and flute solos; there is one for strings and oboes only; there are others with trumpets and kettledrums. Frequently the cast changes within the work, as when in a symphony with winds, the adagio is written for strings only. In a symphony of 1761 (*Le Matin*) quite a strange movement occurs, called "*recitativo*," where the solo violin plays a complete recitative, accompanied by the other strings—an effect which anticipates the recitatives in Beethoven's sonatas op. 30, No. 2 and op. 110 and in the Finale of the Ninth symphony.

As the cast of the winds varies, so too, their special uses change incessantly. Sometimes they are restricted to the representation of harmony, sometimes they have soloistic importance, sometimes they support the strings, and sometimes they carry on contrasting dialogues with them. There are innumerable examples of all these varieties. Haydn retained this diversity even in later years, especially when, as in his London symphonies, he worked on the fixed basis that has ever since been the foundation of the full orchestra: flutes, oboes, clarinets, bassoons, horns, trumpets, kettledrums, and strings. Never did he use a permanent scheme of orchestration. His instruments were always treated as individuals; they were called upon when necessary, otherwise they were kept silent.

The first violin, of course, represented the leading voice, and the strings always remained the foundation of the whole. All other voices Haydn employed only as he saw fit. His orchestration was always inspired by his alertness to invention and variety. No repetitions are to be found within his works in spite of their large number. He always looked for new effects, and in his later years he himself expressed regret that he had learned the principles of the treatment of the wood-winds only as an old man.

Haydn's melodies, especially those of the slow movements, appear to be imitations of vocal melodies, but actually they have been transformed into true instrumental style. The themes of the fast movements are adapted to the character of the strings, their outlines determined by important tones of the chord, such as the 5th, 3rd, and octave. These tones proved to be the most suitable for instrumental performance, not only for the strings but for the winds as well, which also participate in the execution of these themes. The use of different keys within single movements as well as in the work as a whole, permits the richest display of harmony by such emphasis upon the most important tones.

Haydn's restless spirit of invention served him also in the weaving of programmatic ideas into his music.

We know the famous episodes from the oratorios, from "The Creation" especially with its picture of chaos, its instrumental portrayals of the sunrise and of different animals. Haydn liked such references in his instrumental works also. The symphony called *Le Matin,* previously mentioned for its *recitativo,* was complemented by two other symphonies, *Le Midi* and *Le Soir.* There are many other examples of the employment of similar programmatic ideas, even in such simple illustrative form as when, in the "Farewell" symphony, one player after the other extinguishes his candle and leaves the room—a symbolic request to Prince Esterhazy for leave of absence for the musicians, eager to return to their families in Eisenstadt.

At first sight such programmatic picture-painting seems very naïve, but it proves the flexibility and unaffectedness of Haydn's aesthetic principles. He did what he liked with his orchestra. He felt absolutely secure in the use of all media and he enjoyed this superior playing with them. There was no limit to his fancy. The orchestra had learned to speak with such clearness, that even the spoken word could not surpass the lucidity and aptness of this instrumental language.

6

If Hadyn had brought his orchestra to the pitch of expressing everything he wanted to express, the question arises: what was this "everything"? *In what sort of intellectual atmosphere did Haydn's orchestra come to function, and why had this new medium come into being in place of the old types of musical expression?*

Wagner says that Haydn's symphony represents the idealization of the dance. This is true enough, but only with respect to the third and fourth movements, the minuet and finale. The second movement, Andante, Adagio, even Largo, cannot be included among dance types. It is purely a song type, even in the early symphonies and quartets, and this singing character grew with Haydn's development, particularly after he became acquainted with Mozart's music. Least of all can the first movement be related to dance impulses. Its form represents an intellectual process, often very complicated. The slow introductions, especially those of the later period, reach such solemn pathos, that they discover not the remotest connection with any idea of dance. We must expand Wagner's statement and say: there is no field of human feeling, from the deepest absorption to frolicsome cheer, which Haydn does not cultivate in his music. It is a great mistake to think that he was only the merry old "Papa Haydn," who perhaps gazed occasionally upon more earnest thoughts but then turned quickly back to his amusing fancies.

Certainly—speaking only of the musician—Haydn's was a happy temperament. He cared not for melancholy reflection and vexation of spirit. But this disposition should not be misunderstood. Such cheerfulness is not that of superficiality, it is the serenity of the true artist, whose art stands above all the events of reality. Haydn was of an Anacreontic nature. His appreciation of life was based upon the conviction that this world is founded upon a good and right order which is not to be disturbed even by the suffering of the individual. This classic rationalist ideology assumes a harmonious order of all forces, obedient to the rules of reason. Reason is divine, therefore no contrast exists between religion and reason. God himself is a reasonable being. Accordingly Haydn had no scruples, pious Christian though he was, about becoming a free-mason.

Reason was the highest, the divine standard in personal life and in art. The instrumental language seemed an especially suitable medium for such ideology. It had proved itself capable of representing all human feelings. It was a sublime language, expressing all the experiences of the human heart but reflecting them in an idealized manner, far removed from the exciting reality of words and the human voice. From this point of view instrumental language seemed to be superior to words: the instrument might be described as the voice elevated to a higher degree.

So the instrument, and hence the orchestra, appeared to be the organ of this ruling reason. It embraced all passions, feelings, and emotions, but at the same time it cleansed them of all earthy stains. It was itself organized according to the principle of expediency, and this principle again was ruled by reason.

All this represents quite a clear, perfectly rounded world, which, knowing all human pains and griefs, surmounts them, so that the final picture is of a good, well-ordered world. *Feeling is subordinate to reason.* There is no Faustian distress. Harmony alone is its foundation and its purpose, and all differences must be ironed out.

Such was the inner law of Haydn's art. From it sprang his form, his orchestration, his treatment of the instrument individually and in the mass. This art was in truth a sort of new religion, calling all who sought a new faith. It did not contrast with the former art, but represented it in a more highly developed and purified stage. This new faith spread vigorously. It was at first restricted to small circles of country gentlefolk, as Haydn found them in Weinzierl and Lucavec. With time it reached a larger society in Esterhaz, in Vienna, and in Paris. Finally in London Haydn came into touch with a whole public.

As the circle of his audience thus expanded, Haydn's forms, the compass of his expression and of his orchestral apparatus, were likewise enlarged. The development of the orchestra itself, and quite particularly in the matter of its material support, re-

THE CLASSIC ORCHESTRA

ceived an important impetus from the new works created by Haydn. When he began he found, as we have seen, only small groups of musicians, most of them employed as servants in the aristocratic households. With the increasing cultivation of orchestral music these musicians were kept busy by purely professional activities. Public orchestras were now founded in Germany, and again in the 19th century, for the performance of Haydn's oratorios, much as choral societies were formed in England in the 18th century for the performance of Handel's oratorios.

So, Haydn became the leading and the representative composer of his time, admired and celebrated throughout the world, in France as well as in Germany, Austria, and England. His personal life and his art were not disturbed by this acknowledgment. On the contrary, all such outward events seemed to be but external fulfillments of the inner laws that governed Haydn's creative work, as they governed the intellectual atmosphere of his time: feeling ruled by reason, music ruled by harmony, harmony represented by the instrumental symphony—all in all a hymn to *rationalism* as the highest manifestation of human productivity, ruled by divine enlightenment.

III

The Opera Orchestra of *Mozart*

I

While the concert orchestra was developing as the new representative of instrumental art, producing new types of musical forms as well as new audiences, a different path was being followed by another branch of orchestra music: the opera orchestra. It was not so independent as the concert orchestra. It was bound to a certain practical purpose: accompaniment of both the singing voices and the action. So that it was generally speaking a secondary, a subordinate factor, at best but one part of a larger whole. This whole imposed various limitations upon its separate parts and especially upon the orchestra. General conditions had to be considered and more especially the particular requirements of the voice. Consequently the story of opera reveals with time a growing struggle between the voices and the orchestra. But on the other hand this very regard for the voices and the action proved to be a stimulus to creative invention which carried over into the development of orchestral music of purely instrumental style.

THE OPERA ORCHESTRA

This was true not only in the forms of composition and the use of the instruments but also in the development of orchestral technique and ensemble discipline—a new art, regulated by new rules of musical coöperation. The creation of an instrumental unit demanded other principles of organization and preparatory study than the chorus. The chorus remains a union of individual but homogeneous voices, joined in a common purpose. An instrumental body, however, is made up of instruments of heterogeneous kinds, which must sacrifice their individualities in the creation of a new super-individual instrument. It was necessary to cover over the numerousness of the individual performers, to transform them into mechanical players like the registers of the organ or the keys of the harpsichord.

This important task called for a new leading personality endowed with the competence to handle such educational work: the conductor. The first musician to perceive this problem and solve it by a fundamental method was Jean Baptiste Lully, court conductor to Louis XIV of France and director of the royal opera in Paris. Through his dictatorial position he had the authority to discipline the royal orchestra, the "violons du roi." Through his abilities as a composer he became the founder of French opera, basing it upon the models of Monteverdi's Italian opera. Through his close knowledge of all branches of music—he was himself a violinist, an actor and a dancer

—he evolved in his treatment of the instrumental body at his command the true organic form of that unity known as the modern opera orchestra.

Originally the opera orchestra, as employed in the first opera performances by the Florentine amateurs, was placed beside the stage, where it was invisible, in keeping with its primitive duty as a group of accompanying strings. Monteverdi, the first great musician to write opera in Venice, increased the importance of the orchestra by the use of organ, trombones, and cornets in addition to the strings with theorbos, harp and cembalo. Monteverdi's orchestra, famous because of the first employment of the instrumental tremolo, was still limited to accompaniment. The overture, the only opportunity for independent orchestral display, had not yet been made use of. An opera began with either a sung prologue or a short instrumental prelude, as in Monteverdi's *Orfeo* (1607), at the beginning of which a simple fanfare-like toccata in C major was played three times over.

2

MONTEVERDI had two successors in opera composition: the North-Italian Lully and the South-Italian Alessandro Scarlatti. Lully early went to Paris and advanced quickly to the position of court composer. Scarlatti founded a new school of opera composition in Naples, the development of which lay in the unfolding of the virtuosity of the voices, so that here

THE OPERA ORCHESTRA

again the orchestra was restricted to accompaniment. French opera, however, was based upon a mixture of dancing and singing. In consequence of the peculiar conditions imposed by the language and by the nature of the voices it had to work with, the French singing style avoided all tendencies toward virtuosity. It was limited to songs and declamatory recitatives. Both this emphasized dramatic character and the dances inserted as an essential ingredient of the whole, necessarily predetermined to some extent the rôle of the orchestra in French opera. Lully was the ideal person to take up this orchestra, to develop the type of music it called for, to instruct its players, and generally to mold it into a component part of opera on the same level with singing and dancing.

The dances provided the first opportunity for the independent unfolding of the orchestra, independent, at least, of words. Besides developing the music for these dances, Lully created the overture, a composition written, as we know, for orchestra only and as prelude to the opera. Lully's overture consisted of two slow movements separated by a lively section written in fugue-style. This was the so-called French overture. With time it was combined with the dances and performed apart from the opera as an independent orchestral work, known as the French suite.

Scarlatti in Naples also felt the necessity for an instrumental introduction to opera. But he chose the opposite arrangement: he put a slow middle-movement between two lively movements and called the whole a "sinfonia." The French form emphasized the pathetic character of this piece, the Italian form the light introductory character, the slow parenthesis being for the sake of contrast. Both forms influenced the subsequent development of the overture, but from the beginning the French form represented the higher artistic type because of its marked seriousness, while the Italian sinfonia remained an informal improvisation. The French overture reflected the higher standard and greater importance attributed to the orchestra in accordance with the peculiar character of French opera.

Lully was the very man for the education of an orchestra for such music. A despotic character, imperious as an absolute sovereign, he directed his band by pounding out the rhythm with a large baton, just as to-day the beginning of a play is announced at a French theatre. A legend tells that Lully's fatal illness resulted from an injury to his foot while conducting in this manner. Such conducting may seem clumsy to us, rude even. But considering the nature of dance music and the marked rhythmic accents of French opera music, the stressing of the chief notes by knocks of a baton may not have been so disturbing as at first appears. At all events, it was a reliable method for achieving exactness and unification of the instruments.

In Italy, and so also in Germany, the opera con-

THE OPERA ORCHESTRA

ductor—usually the composer—indicated the rhythm from his seat at the cembalo, where he accompanied the recitatives. This less noisy but also less exact method of keeping the instruments together came about partly through the Italian *secco* recitatives, accompanied by the cembalo only. French opera did not employ these "dry" recitatives; hence the cembalo was not an essential part of its orchestra, and the loose method of conducting from the cembalo could be replaced by the exactness of the pounding baton. Another method was to conduct with the bow from the first desk of the violins, but this became customary only in the concerts. This was the method Haydn chiefly used in Eisenstadt; later, in London, he took his seat at the cembalo. This practice assumed a certain confidence in the reliability of the players. The French method was clearer, more military, and because of its exactness laid the foundation of modern orchestral discipline.

From its original location beside the stage, the orchestra was gradually moved to the front of the stage. Probably our use of the term *orchestra*, which originally meant the place where the Greek chorus was gathered, came from this seating arrangement. But did not this orchestra disturb the dramatic illusion with its desk lights and the ugly business of the players? It is characteristic that this problem also was first considered in France. It was a Frenchman, more exactly a Belgian living in France, François Grétry, who—without any reference to the primitive Florentine arrangement—discussed in his writings the idea of an orchestra invisible to the audience. Born in 1742, about 50 years after Lully's death, Grétry died in 1813, the birth-year of Wagner, who was destined to realize Grétry's visions.

The French were, on the whole, the first to develop practical orchestral technique in every respect. Lully was the most important organizer of the orchestra and administered all its affairs, artistic and practical. His model in the European social state was the absolute monarchy of that time, represented by the mighty personality of Louis XIV. Just as Louis and his methods of ruling became typical for all the political, social, and artistic activities of the European states, so, Lully's orchestra, the first example of a well-ordered instrumental ensemble, set the model for other European court orchestras, in opera at first, but in the course of time, and especially through the influence of its artistic standard, for the growing concert orchestras also.

3

The Lully tradition naturally developed most fruitfully in France. Rameau, Lully's successor, was already employing (around 1750) the orchestral cast that Beethoven used fifty years later. Even clarinets were used occasionally. The growth of the opera orchestra was not dependent only upon purely artistic considerations, however. The action in opera also influenced the organization of the orchestra. It sometimes required unusual instruments, like the trombones, use of which in the concert orchestra was not customary. When Gluck wanted to portray an oracle, the sacred sound of the trombones proved to be the only instrumental color suitable to the words of the singing god, as they were to the voices of the *dieu infernau* in *Alceste*. A similar need induced Mozart to employ the trombones in *Don Giovanni*, where they characterize the appearance of the commander's ghost, and in *The Magic Flute* where they represent the solemn calls of the priests.

The action was responsible for the occasional use of certain percussion instruments, too, to represent a primitive touch, as in the portrayal of the Scyths in Gluck's *Iphigenia in Taurus* or the naïve sound of Papageno's bells in *The Magic Flute*. Other instruments were called for by descriptive episodes in the text, as where in Gluck's *Armida* Rinaldo mentions singing birds and murmuring wells when he enters Armida's magic garden. Thus every episode on the stage justified an expansion of orchestral expression, a utilization of the illustrative qualities of the instruments. The musical description of a revolt or of an escape or of any surprise induced the opera composer to discover instrumental effects which illustrated such events.

This tendency to utilize the pictorial possibilities of

the instruments increased in proportion with the tendency toward realistic interpretation of the action. Thus also the importance of the instruments grew in the same measure that the style of singing favored the realistic rendering of the words instead of a predominantly vocalistic exploitation of the voice. Dynamics also were included in this utilization of instrumental effects for dramatic purposes. The illustration of a thunderstorm or of an approaching and then receding crowd—like the famous Turkish patrol in Grétry's *Two Misers*—was a welcome opportunity for the use of crescendo and decrescendo. Astonishment, caused by some unexpected incident, could be dramatically expressed by either a sudden piano or a sudden forte. A slowly growing crescendo, on the other hand, proved the natural musical way of making credible a slowly growing excitation, while a diminuendo would provide a relaxation of the mood.

In this way the events of the action in opera demanded corresponding action by the orchestra. The composers, too, were undoubtedly looking for plots that needed such special orchestral effects. Probably the two tendencies worked together: the need for orchestral illustration implicit in the action, and on the other hand the desire for an opportunity to employ impressive orchestral effects. No matter from which source the impulse sprang, the essential fact was that a continuous exchange of impulses arose from the coöperation of the singing and acting with the orchestra. All parts profited from this reciprocal process, but the greatest advantage went to the orchestra, for its wealth of expressiveness was thus revealed. In the process the orchestra acquired a steadily increasing vocabulary which could be utilized also apart from opera, independent of the restrictions of the stage. The later development of opera called forth such an extraordinary growth in the orchestra that by degrees the servant became the master, a despot, even, who tyrannized over all the other elements of this art-form.

4

But the most important influence upon the orchestra in opera proceeded not from the action and the plot, but from the immediate and indissoluble connection with the singing voice. It was this connection which kept instrumental melody from losing itself in a merely abstract style, a danger which arose the moment the instrument was left to its own devices. Instrumental melody could not have existed, indeed, only as imitation of sung melody. It was bound to discover its independence because of the particular capacities of the instruments, in some ways more restricted, in some ways further reaching than those of the voice.

It for a long time—even after the foundations of independent instrumental technique had been laid—instrumental expression clung to the models supplied by the voice, the instrument in return also had its influence upon the development of the voice. The two were dependent one on another. The voice could unfold more freely and easily upon the background furnished by the instrument, the instrument drew inexhaustible stimulus and encouragement from the voice. It seemed best to let them work together in such a way that neither was subordinate to the other but both were on the same level, complementary to one another.

These conditions found expression in the form of opera as soon as the instrumental body had passed the stage of mere accompaniment and risen to partnership and free interchange with the voice, responding to it by imitating, completing, or contradicting, now subdued to give the voice free play, now taking the lead on its own account. Thus the instrument kept in touch with the origins of melodic style and was saved from losing itself in purely rhythmic, dynamic, coloristic, or technical effects and from dying out through forgetfulness of song.

At this point the importance of *Mozart* to the development of the opera orchestra becomes paramount. The whole line of opera composers, of course, from Monteverdi to Lully, Scarlatti, Handel, Hasse, Rameau, Gluck, and many others, followed a similar path, but Mozart was representative of them all. His works belong to a period when the orchestra was achieving a position of dominance. Haydn had created

THE OPERA ORCHESTRA

a special orchestral style and musically his instrumental works constituted an equal or even a superior counterpart to opera. Indeed there was no danger that the symphony might supersede the opera, so no competition existed between them. But the question now suggested itself, how could the new symphonic style be utilized by opera? And would both, opera and symphony, derive fresh impetus from the combination?

Mozart was not by nature inclined to the primarily instrumental quality of symphonic conceptions. Despite his familiarity with all the instruments and his virtuosity at the piano, his musicianship was always conditioned by the medium of singing. He knew the principle of thematic development, but Haydn's rational kind of symphonic thinking was not his. This abstract intellectual method of shaping music seemed to him applicable only if the fundamental singing character of music was nevertheless retained. His instrumental and even his symphonic themes were not analogous to Haydn's, built up from short triad motives, suitable for symphonic development. Mozart's themes always attest to their singing origin. They are primarily melodic, and accordingly they proceed more by the repetition of the different melodic phrases, than the working-out of the motives. Even when Mozart used contrapuntal forms, as in the final fugue from the so-called "Jupiter" symphony or in the Allegro from *The Magic Flute* overture, the taking to pieces of the theme is directed by the intent to sustain a continuous melodic line. The analytical impulse of the instrumental composer is always controlled by the synthetic impulse of the vocal composer.

5

IT IS a strange fact, particularly significant in the historical development of music, that Mozart's life was enclosed by Haydn's life. When Mozart was born in 1756, Haydn was already 24 years old. In later years they met in Vienna and each esteemed the other highly. Perhaps they felt that their creative works sprang from different sources and radiated in different directions, so that each could without envy admire the other and learn from him. Mozart received from Haydn a new conception of the orchestra as a whole, of the tonal effects and the logic of form possible to the instrumental ensemble, and he carried this stimulus into his own work. Indeed the influences of Haydn on Mozart did not take the form of imitation, but were amalgamated as a matter of course with the melodic style of Italian tradition which both composers had inherited.

The cast and the special technique of Mozart's orchestra represent no such innovations as Haydn's. In his serenades, notturnos, symphonies, Mozart, like Haydn, employed those instruments which were at hand. Mozart's last symphonic works show the setting

THE OPERA ORCHESTRA

usual at that time: strings, flutes, oboes or clarinets, bassoons, trumpets, horns, kettledrums, each of the winds in pairs. Not the technique, only Mozart's manner of handling his orchestra produced its particular character. This manner sprang from his ability to reveal each instrument as a singing and acting individuality, an ability he had acquired and developed in his experience with the opera orchestra. In opera each instrument had to display its special power in competition or in contrast with the human voice. The opera orchestra demanded ready wit, epigrammatic brevity, the power instantaneously to characterize a personality or a situation, a dramatic event or a special mood. This task paralleled the new ideal of opera in general, aiming at realistic representation of the action, as in Mozart's *Abduction, Figaro, Don Giovanni, Cosí fan tutte, The Magic Flute.* The acting characters were no longer mythical beings, singing improbably-worded arias. They were real personalities, expressing their feelings in a natural musical way.

Accordingly the instruments were needed to illustrate words, moods, feelings. Tamino's flute, Papageno's bells, the Turkish rhythms of Osmin, Don Giovanni's mandolin, even the trombones of the Commander were required by the action. Other instrumental effects were called for by lyric moments, as, for example, the singing of the oboe and bassoon in the letter-duet of the countess and Susanna in *Figaro,* the expressive solo oboe in Pamina's aria from *The Magic Flute*. One of Mozart's favorite instruments was the clarinet. Because of its resemblance to the human voice, he used it frequently for answering the singer's melody, or for particularly solemn moods, such as those in the scene between the speaker and Tamino, and when the three mysterious pages are mentioned. Mozart especially favored the basset-horn, a kind of alto-clarinet, the earnest, sombre tones of which he employed in several of his last works, most strikingly in *The Magic Flute*.

Oboe, bassoon, flute, even horns and trumpets take their places at suitable moments, illustrating the dramatic situation with characteristic phrases that correspond to the emotions of the singers and the special qualities of the instrument concerned. Thus the piccolo illustrates Monostatos' lascivious greed. Comic hints, too, appear, as when in his jealousy aria the horns tease Figaro in allusion to his supposed fate. Yet Mozart used the instruments with striking economy. The first five numbers in *Figaro* are written without clarinets; only in Cherobino's aria does the clarinet first appear, and then flute and oboes are omitted. In general the wind-groups vary. There will be oboes, bassoons, and horns; flutes and clarinets; various other mixtures; only at the most important moments do all the winds join in. So Mozart cast his opera orchestra just as the dramatic situation demanded.

Hence this orchestra was not a fixed ensemble but a society of solo instruments arranged in different combinations. Since each instrument revealed its special character in accordance with the play and the singing, Mozart's orchestra reflected the essential nature of his operas. Like them it represented a union of individualities, comparable to acting characters. The independent individualities of both singing and instrumental voices were developed to their highest productivity. The ensemble effect, as such seemingly left to take care of itself, proved an organic consequence of the inherent rightness of the conception as a whole.

Thus Mozart comparatively seldom utilizes group effects uniting all the wood-winds or all the strings to produce a certain color impression. When he does —as in the string unison at the beginning of the *Figaro* overture—it is only for the purpose of arousing a certain tension preparatory to the clarification of the separate instrumental voices. Always the tendency is to emancipate voices; each instrument strives to detach itself from the mass and to unfold its individuality. Obviously this tendency finds its most expansive outlet in opera, where stage and orchestra coöperate to the same end. Through it Mozart, gathering up the preparatory threads spun by his predecessors, established the equality of singing and instrumental parts in opera. His orchestra was no longer mainly an accompanying body, but the intimate and complementary partner of the singers.

6

THIS result was summarized in the overture. Originally, as we have seen, the overture was merely a general introduction, an entertaining prelude in the hands of the Italians, a serious preparation for the coming drama in those of the French. But these overtures contained no immediate reference to the opera by anticipation of themes or melodies from the music to follow. Gluck was the first to adopt this idea. In his later works he used several types of overtures. *Orfeo,* the first of his so-called reform-operas, composed in 1762, has no overture; *Iphigenia in Taurus,* his last great opera, written in 1779, has only a short prelude painting the storm which drives Orestes toward the coast of Taurus. In the intervening operas, *Alceste* and *Armide,* Gluck employed the French type of overture, here only a free prelude utilizing no opera themes, but in *Alceste* leading without interruption into the first scene of the opera.

The most famous of Gluck's overtures, however, that from *Iphigenia in Aulide,* shows direct reference to the opera. It begins with a quotation from Agamemnon's prayer in the form of a slow introduction. In the development of the overture itself, indeed, there is still no anticipation of the coming action, but the idea of this action is called up in such a way that

THE OPERA ORCHESTRA

the piece is no longer generally introductory but constitutes a preparatory reference to the opera. The hearer, of course, is not aware of this. The orchestra begins to speak and to hint at the story of the opera by means of suggestions, later explained by the words sung in the first scene.

So Gluck's overture became an organic link of the opera. Mozart continued this principle. Among the overtures of his best known operas that from the *Abduction* shows the Italian structure: fast, slow, fast, the slow movement anticipating Belmonte's first aria, expressing his longing for Constance. The *Figaro* overture is simply a fast movement developed from a general conception of the last finale without striking reference to the opera, and its musical content impresses the hearer mainly as a setting for the intellectual sphere of the action. The *Così fan tutte* overture begins with the music to the title-motto and its form resembles the French overture type.

Mozart consciously employed this French type in the overtures to *Don Giovanni* and *The Magic Flute*, both of which have slow introductions taken from the most impressive moments of the action: in *Don Giovanni* the mystic harmonies of the Commander, in *The Magic Flute* the solemn trombone-calls of the priests. The *Don Giovanni* overture, like Gluck's *Iphigenia in Aulide* overture, connects immediately with the first scene. *The Magic Flute* overture omits the repetition of the slow introduction at the end, having inserted it at an earlier moment, and finishes, as does the opera, with the festive climax of the fugue-allegro.

The important effect of this development of the overture upon the opera orchestra lay not in any principles of form, but in the use of direct musical references to the most significant moments of the action. This innovation showed that the poetic ideas in the action had penetrated into the originally purely musical construction of the overture. Herewith the particular influence of opera upon the development of instrumental language becomes evident. Through continuous association with events in the action and with the emotions of the dramatis personae, through continuous coöperation with the singing voice, the instruments discovered their own expressive language. Now by imitation, now by taking hints from certain formulae of vocal expression, they developed and enlarged their own dynamic and coloristic compass. Beginning to speak still bound to reminiscences or anticipations of certain episodes in the opera itself, the longer they kept connection with the singing voice the clearer and stronger their powers of expression became.

And now the growing consciousness of these powers led to a new aim in opera as well as concert orchestra: the independence of the instruments from the explanatory word without loss of intelligibility or pathos. The word became superfluous; it was refined to an idea, an image in the background. The musical thought was liberated from the restrictions of language and the human voice like a fledgling from its shell. The instrument, fully weaned from vocal models of expression, became anxious to combine what it had drawn from the voice with its own newly discovered abilities.

Haydn had established the independence of the instruments and combined them into a rational unity. Mozart had inspired this orchestral unity with the singing qualities of the human voice. Now Beethoven appeared, to utilize all that Haydn and Mozart had contributed to the orchestral world and conquer the realm of the idea, the new empire of the orchestra.

IV

The Dynamic Orchestra of *Beethoven*

I

Beethoven's orchestra does not appear to differ in principle from Mozart's orchestra and that of Haydn's later period. Besides the strings, which always form its natural foundation, there are the woodwinds, each in pairs, flutes, oboes, clarinets—now permanent members of the woodwind family—and bassoons. Furthermore there are horns and trumpets and kettledrums, likewise in couples. Sometimes Beethoven enlarged this cast. In the Third symphony, the "Eroica," he employed a third horn; in the Ninth symphony a fourth horn and for the second and fourth movements three trombones; in the Fifth symphony, trombones and double-bassoon. In *Fidelio* he used the double-bassoon; the *Fidelio* overture calls for two trombones, the *King Stephen* for four horns and double-bassoon, *Weihe des Hauses* ("Dedication of the House") for four horns and three trombones.

These changes must, however, be regarded only as due to particular reasons; they do not involve funda-

THE DYNAMIC ORCHESTRA

mental differences from the earlier classic orchestra. Beethoven tended to enlarge the number of the strings because of the more marked dynamic effects, although he did not specify an exact number as Berlioz and Wagner did later. Furthermore he was making new demands upon technical efficiency. The hitherto subordinate violas, cellos, and double-basses he frequently used for soloistic purposes, as, for instance, the string basses in the Trio of the Fifth symphony Scherzo or in the famous recitatives of the Ninth. The winds also, woods as well as brasses, were sometimes assigned difficult solos, as the horn in its particularly dangerous solo in the Adagio of the Ninth symphony and the oboe in the recitative-like cadence of the first movement of the Fifth.

The first violins frequently had to play in high positions and the calls on their technical mobility were increased. Of course Beethoven wrote in general more simply in his symphonies than in his quartets. Sometimes, indeed, he increased his demands almost to the point of virtuosity, as in the codas of the second and third *Leonore* overtures with their brilliant string passages, difficult technically as well as in the ensemble playing. But such episodes were on the whole exceptions, extended individual cases. In principle Beethoven never left the foundation of the traditional orchestra of that time. He was not, like Haydn, a conductor. He did not have to work practically with an orchestra, which might have induced him to modify or to restrict his demands. He started from the existing basis and composed in each case in accordance with his own ideas.

The orchestra he needed for his concert performances had to be made up for each event. In the beginning it generally consisted of a mixture of musicians and amateurs, as was usual in the private performances of the aristocracy. With time the amateurs disappeared because of the increased technical difficulties of the music, so that the professional musicians gained the upper hand. The place of performance also changed. The drawing-rooms of the nobility no longer afforded the requisite resonance for an orchestral symphony concert; they were reserved for solo and chamber music. Orchestral concerts became by degrees a public affair, regulated by business interests. This development had begun early in the 18th century. We remember that in England public performances for financial recompense had already been founded in the last quarter of the 17th century, while Handel's oratorios and concerti had formed a new centre for public concerts. When Haydn came to London in 1791 there were already two competing series of orchestral concerts. In Paris the concerts spirituels had existed since 1725. Even in Germany public musical entertainments were arranged—besides the ecclesiastical concerts for the performance of the Passions and other religious music. The travelling virtuosi had introduced public concerts and as

THE DYNAMIC ORCHESTRA

time went on a civic orchestra, consisting mainly of amateurs, would contribute some pieces on these occasions. In Vienna at the end of the 18th century the *Society of the Friends of Music* became the centre of a growing musical life and organized several regular public concerts during the season.

Hence the public performance of Beethoven's works was not a wholly new thing, nor was it unusual as a way for the composer to earn money. What was new, was that Beethoven's works required the public setting as a background against which to display to the full their implicit effects. So these works represented a new kernel around which grew the organization of public concerts. The first performances of the "Eroica," it is true, took place in 1804 in the palace of Prince Lobkowitz, but probably this was only an act of politeness. The performance of the First and Second symphonies had been arranged in 1800 and 1803 in public concerts, the Fourth symphony first appeared in 1807 at a subscription concert, and from then on all the big new works were promptly performed in public, mostly in pairs: the Fifth symphony at the same concert with the Sixth in 1808, the Seventh with the Eighth in 1814, the Ninth in 1824 on the same evening when three movements from the great Mass were performed for the first time. These audiences were not shy of novelties; on the contrary, a concert was considered as offering an opportunity to hear new compositions.

The orchestra was developing, then, both as a group of professional musicians and as a public institution which claimed the attention not only of music-lovers but of all interested persons. This change paralleled the transition from the aristocratic attitude of society in the 18th century to the civic attitude of the 19th century. In the field of music this cardinal turning-point was symbolized by Beethoven's symphony.

2

IT CANNOT be supposed that Beethoven himself was conscious of this fact or that he intentionally included it in the conception of his symphonies. It became manifest simply as the natural and organic consequence of the content and structure of the works themselves. The question arises: What then was, musically speaking, the actual change that took place? From what quality of Beethoven's symphony did it spring, growing to influence not only the musical form but even the character of the audience, of the place, of all the elements involved in the production and its reception—in short, of the performance as a whole?

Apart from the particular attributes of Beethoven's intellect and temperament, the *dynamic quality of his appreciation of music* must be acknowledged as the distinguishing mark of his musicianship. This dynamic sense determined his use of instruments, his perception of musical forms, the development of his ideas. Thus it came also to play a part in all the circumstances surrounding the performance of his compositions.

Dynamics are a manifestation of emotion. In Beethoven's music feeling has broken into the rational structure of Haydn's musical form, the individual tendency of Mozart's. This is its fundamental characteristic. And this expression of feeling was an outburst of new spiritual forces awakened by the stirring events taking place in all fields of human activity, especially by social and political revolution.

Beethoven as a young man had seen the effects of the French Revolution. He sympathized with the new ideas of humanity, cosmopolitanism, liberty, equality, fraternity. But these ideas, the natural consequences of the preceding theories of reason and individualism, could not be realized in a musical medium that was perfectly clear and objective. For they sprang from vague, ungoverned instincts, from emotions that fluctuated with irregular excitations. Their expression in music required a similarly irregular rise and fall of line, calling forth no rational concreteness of form but a more indefinite, flowing motion, and aiming not at well-defined objectivity but at continual awareness of the incessant fluctuation of emotional excitation.

For this purpose the dynamic element in music was the best possible medium, and the development of dynamics in the most widely-varying directions must be recognized as Beethoven's main objective. From this point of view, Beethoven opened the 19th century as the first of what we call the romantic composers. But his dynamic romanticism was always governed and directed by the great inheritance of the 18th century, by the rationality of Haydn's classicism, the individualism of Mozart's. When the unchecked dynamic element threatened to burst all dikes, reason and rational individualism would recognize the limits and by their subduing powers prevent an overflowing of the banks. This self-control characterized Beethoven's particular importance and greatness. His belonging to the 18th century was confirmed by the fact that, though a dynamic nature and filled with dynamic instincts, he always respected the limits of rational perception. Thus he succeeded in creating a balance between reason and feeling, between form and dynamics. Thus, too, he became the last classicist and the first romanticist, summarizing the activities of the preceding age and transposing them into the new age, dominating both periods as a superior creator who increased the forces of the past by drawing on the still unreleased powers of the future.

3

THESE general qualities of Beethoven's musicianship explain how and why instrumental music inevitably became his main field of activity. He did compose songs, an oratorio, cantatas, two masses, and even an opera. But while they represent only a by-group among his works, the interior organization of even these compositions is based upon the laws and the carrying capacity of their instrumental sections. The instruments are no longer restricted to accompaniment or to stimulating exchanges with the singing voices. These voices themselves become instruments. They may be called Leonore or Florestan or Pizarro, they may sing the words of the Mass or a hymn of joy or in praise of conjugal love, but the form of their singing is always given by the laws that govern instruments.

The most representative of Beethoven's works, however, are his purely instrumental compositions. They divide into three groups: the *piano* works, the *orchestral* compositions, and the *chamber music*. This classification seems to have some general similarity with that of Haydn's works, but there are several important differences. "The Creation" and "The Seasons" represent in a way the crowning of Haydn's creative activity and an organic coördination of the singing voices with the orchestra. Beethoven's orchestra, on the contrary, completely predominates and the voices exist only in subordination to the instruments. Haydn's piano compositions were only a preparation for his chamber and orchestral music. For Beethoven, who began his career as a piano virtuoso, this instrument always preserved its importance as his most personal and intimate medium, even when he himself could no longer play because of his deafness. Haydn, whose orchestra grew up from the string quartet, wrote for this chamber-music group as a study, so to speak, for his orchestral compositions, which represented the acme of his productivity. For Beethoven chamber music was no longer the first step to the orchestra. It was, on the contrary, a kind of last consequence, a sublimated essence of the orchestra. The quartets represent about the same sphere of ideas as the orchestral works, but may be said to deal with these ideas on a higher and more detached plane. Even the dynamic elements so boldly flung forth in the orchestral works and dealt with no less characteristically in the subtle medium of the quartet, being here refined down, as it were, to the very essence of the spiritual impulses they express.

Beethoven's orchestral works cannot be called the foundation of his creative activity, this being the piano sonatas; nor its culmination, this lying in the quartets. But they take their places throughout the whole period of his creative maturity. The chronology of his orchestral compositions shows that they were written between 1800 and 1824, that is between his 30th and 54th years. This fact remains, whatever significance we may to-day read into his preoccupation with the great quartets up to his death—a circumstance which need in no way imply that he considered his orchestral labors over and done with.

The list of Beethoven's orchestral works embraces three groups: the works for orchestra alone; the works for voices and orchestra, including *Fidelio*, the two masses, the oratorio "Christus am Oelberg" (Mount of Olives), and several cantatas, among them "Der Glorreiche Augenblick" (The Glorious Moment), written for performance during the festivities marking the Congress of Vienna in 1814; furthermore the works for a solo instrument with orchestra, such as the five piano concertos and the violin concerto. There exists besides that singular composition "Wellington's Victory or the Battle of Vittoria," written in 1813 for orchestra and projected for the panharmonium of Maelzel, the inventor of the metronome—an odd work because of the gun-shot and other conventional battle-music effects represented in it. It was one of Beethoven's greatest successes and gained him more popularity than all his nine symphonies together. Even more astonishing is the fact that he himself had an exceptionally good opinion of this composition, esteeming it nearly as highly as his symphonies.

This point is worth mention, for it is significant of Beethoven's attitude toward program music. The question, which was to gain such importance in the 19th century, of the artistic admissibility of program music in comparison with so-called absolute music, did not exist for Beethoven. He wrote program music when and where he deemed fit, but rarely for descriptive purpose; a program to him was primarily an outline of states of feeling. Therefore he never considered his programmatic music any less worthy than his other compositions. Nothing mattered to him save the special idea in question, his own purpose in each case.

We are indeed obliged to admit the presence of programmatic ideas in much of Beethoven's music, and not only in such obvious cases as the "Battle of Vittoria" or the "Pastoral" symphony, or the "Les Adieux" sonata, or the *Egmont, Coriolanus,* 2nd and 3rd *Leonore* overtures. Occasional programmatic headings occur in works without programs, as, for example, in the quartet opus 18; no. 6, a movement entitled *"La Malinconia,"* or in the great A minor (op. 132), the *"Canzona di ringraziamento in modo lidico offerta alla divinità da un guarito"* ("A convalescent's song of thanks to the deity in the Lydian mode"); or again such indications for the effects desired as *"ermattend"* ("growing weary") or *"sentendo nuova forza"* ("feeling new strength"). Furthermore, nearly all the indications Beethoven gives are something intermediate between the usual dynamic signs and programmatic remarks. These instructions gradually increase throughout his works both in number and in refinement of gradation. If we should put together those from a single one of the later piano sonatas or quartets we would have a kind of detailed story, in terms of dynamics only, but obviously the residue of a clear train of ideas.

4

The truth is that the usual distinction between program and programless music does not apply to Beethoven. All music was for him a matter of dynamics; only his way of expressing his directions for the display of the dynamic impulse varied. Sometimes they crystallized into concrete conceptions, sometimes they were refined into abstract ideas, inexpressible in words. Sometimes the concrete and abstract were mixed, as when he entitled a symphony "Eroica" but specified nothing further save the heading of the second movement: *"Marcia funebre sulla morte d'un heroe."* A similar process is revealed in the beginning of the last movement of the Ninth symphony: the themes of the three preceding movements are quoted and after some measures each of them is rejected by the recitatives of the double-basses. Then the melody of the hymn of joy sounds and the double-basses themselves take it up. The sketches, preserved by happy accident, prove that Beethoven in composing wrote words of his own invention below the bass recitatives to discover the right and natural declamation. Consequently the programmatic nature of this episode is beyond all doubt.

There has been much violent argument to determine whether Beethoven's program music is genuine program music or whether its titles are merely a convention, whether his works were inspired by and developed from poetic ideas or only from the musical organism itself. Both interpretations seem to be wrong as far as they suppose a contrast between poetic idea and musical organism and pretend that the root of Beethoven's creative impulse must be revealed from either the one or the other. But Beethoven's creative impulse was always derived from sensory excitation. From this dark and mysterious ground it grew up into the light of clarified form to become "expression of feeling rather than portrayal," as he wrote in the score of the "Pastoral" symphony. The force that guided this process and determined the direction of its development—as we observe it to some extent in the sketch books—may be called the idea, even the "poetic idea." *This poetic idea was indeed nothing more than the dynamic impulse taking form.* Therefore the term "poetic idea" refers not to a specific poetic conception but to a general intellectual consciousness that permeated Beethoven's music.

This does not mean that Beethoven tried to imitate the methods of a poet. He knew that the creative process in music was directed by laws similar to those which govern any poetic endeavor: Working from the subconsciousness to the consciousness, from the darkness of feeling to the clearness of plastic objectivity, from the night of primitive emotions in revolt to the triumph of intellectual achievement. In principle this is the way of every creative process. But neither Bach nor Handel nor Haydn nor Mozart had

THE DYNAMIC ORCHESTRA

taken this process itself as their main objective. Their work, following artistic principles of an earlier day, began after this clarification had been finished. In Bach's portrayal of the death and resurrection of Christ, or Haydn's of the change from the chaotic night into the new day, there were sudden and abrupt contrasts of two incompatible elements. But Beethoven took *the transition itself as the object of his art.* In this he is comparable to Rembrandt, who likewise made the stages between light and dark his object and in this fundamental act achieved the particularly stirring and live effect of his painting.

Now the process of transition is a dynamic process. The requirements for its performance determined Beethoven's forms on the whole as well as his choice and treatment of the instruments. They also determined his instructions for the execution of the music in all their variety, and even the occasional formulating of definite programs. These programs were in truth nothing but instructions for the execution, manifestations of the driving dynamic impulse. All these together: forms, instruments, instructions for execution (whether in musical terms or in programmatic words) modelled the dynamic figure so clearly, that it appeared as the unmistakable realization of the creative intent.

In accordance with the different fundamental idea in each case, Beethoven employed different methods for realizing his intent. The C minor symphony shows one of the simplest. It is built firstly upon contrasts of minor and major, secondly upon contrasts of weak and strong dynamics. The second effect produces the climax, and was therefore reserved until the second half of the work. But what an astonishing and grandiose transition is displayed here! There is no systematic and steady rising of the crescendo; instead, the pianissimo is kept and carried along for a great many bars. This raises the tension to an extreme degree of excitement until the final crescendo breaks forth and bursts into the C major fortissimo. This effect is caused only by some held tones of the basses, some beats of the kettledrum, and a slowly rising phrase of the violins. The symphony is famous because of its development from a small thematic kernel, which is carried through from the first to the third and fourth movements. The combination of these two movements and the return of the third within the last is one of the finest manifestations of Beethoven's genius. Yet the whole construction is subordinate to the fundamental dynamic impulse, so that all these striking features are to be regarded not as ends in themselves but as media for the realization of the original dynamic idea.

It is necessary to remember that thematic work as Haydn used it and Mozart's individual treatment of the instruments lost their peculiar importance with Beethoven. They did not disappear, but were melted down, dissolved in the predominating dynamic element, their use depending upon their qualification for dynamic purposes. The variety of these dynamic purposes included not only crescendos like those of the C minor symphony or the codas of the *Egmont* or *Leonore* overtures. Other examples show only the intensive prolongation of a single sustaining dynamic force, as in the last movement of the A major symphony, where there are indeed gradations within the movement, but these are only episodes inserted to prepare for a new climax of the dionysiac base-line. Still other conceptions—as in the second movement of the same symphony—start from a slow mood, rising to a great display and then going back to the starting-point. It is not the passing from piano to forte or vice versa that interests Beethoven, but the incessant variation of light and shadow. *It is just this changeableness that permeates the whole structure,* producing forms not fixed in mold but of living mobility and constantly changing expression.

5

FROM this condition sprang one of the few innovations Beethoven introduced into the symphonic organism: the replacement of the minuet by the scherzo. Haydn's minuet as well as Mozart's seemed too subdued in rhythm, too moderate, insufficient to meet Beethoven's variable demands for vitality. So he loosened the tight rhythms, the melodic periods which had been restricted to the simply contrasting movements of the dancing groups stepping formally towards each other. Instead, breaking away from the illusion of a conventional dance form, and giving free vent to the course, climax and crash of dynamic periods, he invested this movement with the character of an elemental outburst. Even the First symphony reveals this new type; the Third continues along the same line. The scherzi of the Second, Fourth, Sixth, and Seventh symphonies, less demoniacal, still bear a free and transporting dance character. The glory of them all is the Scherzo of the Ninth with its furious opening strokes, its solo kettledrums, its fugual development for strings and its gradual augmentation toward the wild horn-calls, which then in the Trio change to a soft pastoral melody. This whole movement, flashing in its flexibility, is an especially magnificent manifestation of the dynamic conception.

Thus the dynamic impulse determined not only Beethoven's use of instruments and of thematic development, but his construction of the single movement as well as of the form of the whole. Such display of dynamic possibilities brought about a great broadening of the works, since only large compass could give room to such developments. This caused difficulties for the first audiences. They could not appreciate such spacious construction nor discover at once the laws that governed its creation. Beethoven himself seems to have felt the necessity for a certain self-restraint, because after the Third, which was his

THE DYNAMIC ORCHESTRA

boldest conception even in dimension, he endeavored to limit the breadth of his symphonies. From the Fourth to the Seventh they show this restraint, the Fifth striving for an almost epigrammatic brevity, while the "Pastoral" seems long chiefly owing to the slowness of its tempi. The Eighth symphony is a conscious reference to earlier models—a modern composer would have entitled it "in the old style."

Only the Ninth, finished twelve years after the Eighth, again shows monumental enlargement of all proportions. It surpasses even the "Eroica" in the architectural disposition of its three instrumental movements as well as in its employment of solo voices and chorus for the Finale. Beethoven's symphonies are in general vastly proportioned in comparison with those of his predecessors, which may explain why he wrote only 9, while Mozart wrote 41 and Haydn 104. The content of the individual symphonies, too, differs as much as the forms themselves. It does not follow a consistent scheme, but proves in each case to be based upon the expansive force inherent in the fundamental dynamic impulse.

6

Two basic considerations determined the construction of Beethoven's symphony: first, the general type of the movements as reflected in their formal structure and their character of tempo; second, the central tonality and the relations of the keys within the work.

Beethoven found a symphony consisting of four parts —Allegro, Andante or Adagio, Minuet, Allegro (Finale)—this being the type derived from the Italian sinfonia or overture: fast, slow, fast, later completed by the addition of the minuet. He did not change this type in principle, save to replace the minuet by the scherzo, only the Eighth symphony, with its "old style" keeping the minuet. But in the Ninth symphony he changed the succession of the movements by putting the Scherzo in second and the Adagio in third place. Otherwise Beethoven did not deviate from the traditional form. But the more the individual character of the movements was varied. The slow introduction to the first movement—reminiscent of the French overture and already employed by Haydn—was sometimes enlarged so that it had nearly the importance of an independent movement, as in the Second, Fourth and Seventh symphonies. But this was no rule. In the Fifth, Sixth, and Eighth symphonies there is no introduction and in the Third it is limited to only two measures establishing the tonality. The introduction of the Ninth is organically combined with the movement that follows and provides the source of the main theme.

Beethoven's first movement retains in general the sonata form, but with many deviations. In the "Eroica" a third theme is introduced, the development is considerably extended, a second development is inserted. His coda, originally only a short conclusion,

THE DYNAMIC ORCHESTRA

grows into a new organic climax. His second movements differ widely in form, favoring the song type with variations. But the character of this song is different in each work, varying from the simple melodious Andante of the First symphony to the Adagios of the Second and Fourth and the idyllic brook-scene of the "Pastoral," and including the *Marcia funebre* of the "Eroica," the Allegretto of the Seventh, and finally the grand Adagio of the Ninth, a combination of two alternating chains of variations.

His last movement appears in the most important deviations. Originally the finale was a rondo, to a certain extent light music, derived from the dance, heading toward a joyous ending. Sometimes Beethoven kept this ground plan, as in the First, Second, Fourth, Seventh and Eighth symphonies; but even then he altered it with a powerful climax, so that the finale departed from its traditional character and became a musical high-point. In the Fifth symphony this high-point acquires the character of a triumphal solution of the preceding tension, its special gradation being due to the organic connection with the scherzo and its inserted repetition. The most original of Beethoven's finales are those of the "Eroica" and the Ninth. Written in the form of variations, they both develop to a greatness which puts them at least on a par with the first movements, heretofore the most important of the four. The effect they produce, indeed, actually surpasses even that of the first movements, leading up to a great final climax in which all the forces of musical intensity are unchained.

In these different forms from which Beethoven built up his symphonies we see once more the influence of the dynamic impulse. It determines the form on the whole, it determines likewise the character of the single movements. The former symphony had symbolized a solution, a passing from the principal (first) movement, through the lyric intensity of the slow (second), with increasing lightness through the minuet to the finale. Mozart provided some exceptions, as in the "Jupiter" symphony, though even here the finale is only a festive ending, and in the G minor symphony, the Finale of which is certainly no solution but a continuation of the preceding parts in a more passionate and restless mood. But Beethoven's finales open up a new field. They represent a conscious new turn, *a climax attainable only through the inspiring impetus of the dynamic element, which thus created the inner alliance of all the movements as well as the special importance of the concluding finale.*

7

THIS organic unity in the formal structure is accentuated and confirmed by the relations of the keys. We know that Beethoven laid great emphasis on the significance of tonality; he did not like transposition even at the piano. We know also that the significance of the keys was one of the articles of faith in the aesthetics of the time. Let us see how this principle is reflected in Beethoven's orchestral music and how it is to be accounted for.

In general, the first, third (scherzo) and last movements of Beethoven's symphonies are written in the main key. Only when the first movement is in minor does the finale replace minor by major, as in the Fifth and Ninth. The slow movement deviates from the main key, in some cases being written in the dominant (Second symphony), subdominant (First, Sixth and Eighth symphonies), in the relative (minor, "Eroica," major Fifth and Ninth), or in the tonic minor (Seventh symphony). Apparently Beethoven adhered to no regular principle in his choice of key for the slow movement. One wonders whether he adhered at all to any definite principle even in the main keys of the symphonies: two of them are in C (First and Fifth), two in D (Second and Ninth), one in E-flat (Third), one in B-flat (Fourth), two in F (Sixth and Eighth), and one in A. Among the most important overtures we discover the *Prometheus,* the three *Leonores,* the *Coriolanus* and *Weihe des Hauses* written in C, the *Egmont* in F, the *Fidelio* in E. Does there exist an aesthetic relation between the choice of key and the character of the composition? We may think that in Beethoven's mind F-major had an idyllic meaning because he used it in the "Pastoral" and Eighth symphonies. But he also used it in the *Egmont* overture, which can by no means be regarded as an idyllic subject. Indeed no reason can be found for F being any more idyllic than E or D or C.

Consideration of all the symphonies and overtures would yield the same result: not the least difference can be discovered among the single keys so far as any inherent significance is concerned. But there is a decided difference when it comes to performance by the instruments. The mechanical construction of instruments, especially of the strings and brasses, distinguishes their tones into open and covered tones. The more the open tones are employed, the more the individual qualities of the instrument are revealed, whereas the covered tones produce a more artificial and less characteristic effect. Consequently it had been very usual to write symphonies in D, this being the most favorable key for the strings (tuned C-G-D-A-E), which at that time constituted the main body of the orchestra. Haydn, writing a string quartet movement in F-sharp, was apparently interested in avoiding open strings.

With the growing use of the winds other keys came to be employed, namely those in which, because of their mechanical construction, the winds in question sounded most effective. The tone E-flat is not in itself the least bit more heroic than the tone E, but the horn sounds particularly well in E-flat, the characteristic tone-quality of the instrument producing a peculiarly heroic type of expression. Because of this particular capacity of the horn for making the tones related to E-flat, this key seemed to be the most suitable for conveying a heroic conception. Similarly, C is not more triumphant than C-sharp, but C is the tone most natural to the mechanism of the trumpets. The trumpets being the best instruments for victorious and festive expression, the key of C is selected for compositions with a triumphal trumpet culmination such as the Fifth symphony and the *Leonore* overtures.

The choice of keys then, is not primarily dependent on the individual taste or an arbitrary act of the composer, but is conditioned by the character of those instruments which satisfy the actual dynamic needs. These dynamic needs, again, spring from the conception in the composer's mind. To Beethoven, the sound of the horn seemed the most suitable medium for creating an atmosphere of heroic feeling. Therefore he built the "Eroica" upon the sound of the horn, and because E-flat major is the most favorable key for the horn, E-flat became the key of the "Eroica." In like manner, to Beethoven the sound of the trumpet seemed the most suitable medium for creating an atmosphere of triumph. Therefore he built the Fifth symphony and the *Leonore* overtures with the sounds of the trumpets in mind, and because C is the most favorable key for trumpet effects, C became the key for the Fifth symphony and those triumphal overtures. Examples of this sort are numerous. In every case they show that Beethoven's choice of keys in his orchestral works derived from the tonal sphere of the dominant instruments.

Not only the key, but the structure of Beethoven's themes themselves were thus derived from the particular qualities of the instruments. In this field the advancement of the winds was the most influential factor. Haydn's and Mozart's themes were in most cases string themes. They sprang from the technique and the impulse most effectively to display the violins, the wind instruments adding a certain accentuation, but nearly always in such a way that the character of the string theme was preserved. Beethoven's First and Second symphonies represent a similar principle, their musical conception being based wholly upon the string ensemble. But with the "Eroica" the picture changed. The winds became predominant, which means the themes themselves were invented and shaped in such a manner that they might be given their most impressive expression by the winds.

This does not mean that Beethoven's themes were suitable only for winds. The opening themes of the Fifth, Sixth, and Seventh symphonies when played by the strings seem to be string themes, when played by the winds seem to be wind themes. One particularly striking example of this equivocal sonority is the Allegretto from the Seventh symphony. Beginning with the low strings it rises gradually through all registers of the strings and winds, then sinks down

THE DYNAMIC ORCHESTRA

and finally disappears, plucked apart by the different groups. Beethoven's tendency to make themes suitable for strings, wood-winds, or brasses increased with the progress of his work. The Adagio of the Ninth symphony is one of the most perfect examples of this manifold interpretation of instrumental tone.

In spite of his increased use of the winds Beethoven neglected the strings not at all, nor did he restrict them to ornamentation of the winds. They always kept their independence and more especially their rhythmic vitality. The winds meanwhile were no longer only accentuating but absolutely individual voices. Their colors, as we have seen, often determined the character of a movement or of a whole work and gave the mold to the thematic kernel. This dependence on instrumental tone was a primary fact, involved in the dynamic nature of the creative idea. The construction of Beethoven's works is usually regarded as the development of the thematic lines alone, and the orchestration is esteemed but a secondary matter. Surely nobody can demonstrate scientifically which came into existence first in Beethoven's conception, the thematic line or the thought for its instrumental nature. Probably the two grew up simultaneously. But never was the thematic idea conceived alone and in the abstract and afterwards "orchestrated." Any such interpretation would underrate the fundamental importance of instrumental color in Beethoven's orchestra and fail to perceive the influence of dynamics as the creative impulse in his music.

8

THERE is accordingly no basis for believing that Beethoven orchestrated badly, especially in his later years, because of his deafness and his inability to make practical experiments. It is true that Beethoven's orchestration sometimes obscures the clarity of his thematic development. For instance, in the first movement of the Eighth symphony, when the repetition of the main part begins with a dynamic climax, all the instruments sound *fff* in emphatic declaration of F major. Only the double-basses and bassoons take the theme, which of course under such circumstance cannot be heard. But what does this prove? It would be absurd to suppose that after more than 20 years' orchestral experience Beethoven would not have known that the theme could not be heard; on so simple a point he hardly needed trial by experiment. The case only proves that the development not of the thematic but of the dynamic line was most important for him. It seemed to him unnecessary that the theme be heard but necessary that the beginning of the repetition be marked by a mighty triple forte. It is a poor form of arrogance on the part of conductors when they make all the instruments play softly at this point so that the theme of the double-basses can be understood. Such an interpretation destroys the most important effect for the sake of a subordinate one.

The error made in judging most of the so-called badly orchestrated episodes is based upon this sort of misunderstanding of Beethoven's intention, which was always conditioned by the dynamic impetus. From this point of view he employed the instruments, and if in his day the technique of the winds, especially of the horns and trumpets, was still limited to the natural tones, this restriction was not an obstruction to Beethoven. On the contrary, it was a source of new strength. Because from the first he calculated with the natural restrictions, his horns and trumpets especially radiate an elemental brilliance such as has never been heard before or since.

But neither horns nor trumpets nor any other one group of instruments predominates in Beethoven's conceptions. In the introduction of the Fourth symphony, the strings have the heavy unison and the winds only accompany; in the introduction of the Seventh, we see just the reverse picture. Beethoven's instruments have all gained their liberty, all reveal their individualities to the full, all being capable of the same importance in the thematic form and in the symphonic organism as a whole. Here is an orchestra of genuinely democratic constitution, which seems to be not only a medium for but the object itself of symphonic expression. In it Haydn's rational principles of construction and Mozart's unfolding of the individual and singing qualities of the instruments are combined, the creative force of the dynamic impulse amalgamating them into a new unit.

With this new unit the aristocratic and individualistic constitution that had preceded it, became void. All artistic media were now submitted to the rule of the dynamic spirit, gaining thereby a new sense of climax. The music to which this spirit gave expression broke through the earlier limits of form, of sound, of space. It no longer addressed itself to distinct circles, no matter of what quality. It pierced to the very depths of feeling and rose thence upwards toward transcendental perception. Its spiritual attitude, linked with the ideology of liberty, fraternity, and the demand for individual responsibility, perfectly reflected the ideal of liberation of individuality through development of independence, the final goal being unification of all individualities into a free community.

Such was the conclusion expressed in Beethoven's symphonies, in his great mass, in *Fidelio*. Such also the essence of his overtures, whether they end with the real or the imagined triumph of a Leonore or an Egmont or even with the self-destruction of a Coriolanus. The new ideal was not only an artistic, a formal, a social, a political, a religious ideal. It was the summarizing of them all into a new unity, and in the realm of music the organism which embodied

THE DYNAMIC ORCHESTRA

this unity with all its radiations and gave it perfect form was the orchestra. This orchestra has suffered many changes since that time, but never were its cause and purpose brought to such ideal conformity as by Beethoven.

V

The Orchestra of Romantic Illusion:
Weber, Schubert, Mendelssohn, Schumann

I

Beethoven died in 1827, but already several years before his death a new type of orchestra had grown up. It had not only grown up, it was to a certain extent perfected during Beethoven's life-time. Of the three composers who created this new type of orchestra the oldest, Carl Maria von Weber, born in 1786, died as early as 1826, one year before Beethoven. The second, Franz Schubert, born in 1797, survived Beethoven by only one year. The third, Felix Mendelssohn-Bartholdy, born in 1809, lived longer, indeed, until 1847, but had already composed one of his most significant orchestral works, the overture to Shakespeare's *Midsummer Night's Dream*, in 1826. So that the new type of orchestra already existed in its complete form while Beethoven himself was still living and working.

He is even known to have been acquainted with some of the new productions. He knew Weber's

Freischütz and *Euryanthe*, but not *Oberon*, and he knew some of Schubert's compositions, though not the orchestral works. Apparently he was not acquainted with Mendelssohn's compositions. Of course there were other composers cultivating tendencies similar to those of Weber, Schubert, and Mendelssohn, men like Louis Spohr, one of the most famous and highly esteemed musicians of the time and indeed a very important figure both as a violin virtuoso and as a composer of operas, oratorios, and instrumental works. But it was Weber, Schubert, and Mendelssohn who developed and comprehensively summed up all the new ideas. Each of them embodies a special type, and the three together represent in its entirety the musical current known as German romanticism.

Romanticism may be explained from very various points of view: as a flight from reality toward an imaginary world, a world of apparitions, of ghosts and magic forces; as a kind of animating of nature by spirits, fairies, goblins, elfs; as the longing for far exotic countries, inhabited by beings ruled by strange laws; and also as a return to the subconscious fundamentals of the national spiritual life, as manifested in legends of the people's past. Romanticism as a whole represented an outburst of pure emotion, which overflowed all restrictions of reason and rational thinking and unlocked the immeasurable and uncontrollable realm of fantasy.

This attitude, rooted in a deep discontent with the real world and increased by the sense of incapacity to transform that world, spread through every spiritual and artistic field. In music there were three spheres especially suited to the expression of such intentional fictions: song, opera, and orchestral music. Song was the medium for musical enhancement of romantic poetry; opera the medium for visible performance of romantic plots. Orchestra was the medium for the expression of fantastic moods in the mystery of sounds alone, beyond reality. The representative creator for romantic song was Schubert; for romantic opera, Weber; for the romantic orchestra, Mendelssohn. But Mendelssohn stood not alone in his field, for Weber in his operas also needed and developed the romantic orchestra, and Schubert, working from song and piano toward the symphony, likewise contributed much of importance to the new instrumental art. At some distance these three great pioneers were followed by Robert Schumann, the romantic poet of the piano, who, stimulated especially by Mendelssohn, strove to enlarge his own sphere of expression in the direction of the orchestra.

2

THE difference between the romantic orchestra and Beethoven's orchestra at first appears to have been but inconsiderable. The strings remained the backbone of the whole, the wood-winds, flutes, oboes, clarinets, bassoons were employed in pairs, likewise the trumpets. The horns, indeed, which Beethoven used only exceptionally in fours, now almost regularly kept this number, and the trombones became legitimate members of the orchestral family. In general the orchestra of Beethoven's Ninth symphony, for his own uses especially large, was now the normal cast, but this cast was seldom exceeded. The ophicleide, which Mendelssohn called for in the *Midsummer Night's Dream* overture was occasionally used to compensate for the bass tuba, but other variations were scarcely to be found.

The characteristic difference between Beethoven's orchestra and that of the Romantic depends not upon the number and species of the instruments, but upon the nature of their use: their technical treatment as well as the mixture of instrumental colors and the emphasizing of particular tone-qualities. Weber's orchestra especially represented with respect to these qualities a wholly new type and therefore became the model for all romantic composers, and for Mendelssohn, chiefly, who began when Weber died. The *Midsummer Night's Dream* overture was written at the very time that Weber finished his *Oberon* in London. Perhaps the second theme of Mendelssohn's overture, with its striking similarity to the mermaids' song in *Oberon*, was meant to be tribute to the prematurely dead creator of German romantic opera. Schubert, who was about twelve years younger than

Weber, may also have known *Freischütz* and more particularly *Euryanthe*, which was performed in Vienna. Whether and to what degree he was influenced by Weber's conception of orchestral sonority may remain an open question. His own orchestral compositions never came to a practical test in his lifetime, being performed only many years after his death. He had composed them, so to speak, to unbosom himself; they could have exerted no influence upon his contemporaries. Schumann, who discovered the C major symphony ten years after Schubert's death, was the first to use Schubert's orchestral style, but even Schumann had no knowledge of the B minor symphony which did not become known until thirty years later, in 1868.

3

WEBER's first striking departure from the classic orchestra is manifest in the concertante treatment of certain instruments, as opposed to Beethoven's trend to unification. Weber seems to return to an older type of instrumental setting, especially when seen from the standpoint of a later period. He does not gather up orchestral tones into a unity as Beethoven did. He analyzes them and then develops the single voices to a new importance, sometimes by means of virtuosity, sometimes by emphasizing effects which can be produced only by soloistic treatment. Thus he calls special attention to instruments hitherto neglected: the viola, or the clarinet, or the oboe, or the horns. In *Freischütz* he writes a great virtuoso solo for the viola and subsequently for the oboe in Aennchen's humorous tale of the watch-dog Nero. He also makes impressive use of the awesome effect of the viola tremolo or of sustained tones in its low register, as in the slow middle part of the *Euryanthe* overture and in the ravine-scene from *Freischütz*. The clarinet, which Weber knew especially well from his concerts with Baermann, a famous clarinetist of that time, gained a new soloistic brilliance by the development of its singing qualities, as in the famous E-flat major entrance in the *Freischütz* overture. Weber was the first to discover the characteristics of the clarinet's low register, which produces an especially uncanny effect. At the beginning of the ravine-scene from *Freischütz* he writes an F-sharp minor chord, pianissimo, made up of trombones, two low clarinets, and a dark violin and viola tremolo. This was a bold and hitherto quite unknown combination of sounds, reflecting in the sheer gloom of its color the impression of the gruesome landscape. A similar effect proved possible with the low tones of the horns, as for instance, where only the kettledrum and the low horns, all on D, introduce Kaspar's great aria, "Schweig, schweig." Very high tones also provide similarly exciting effects, as the two piccolos in Kaspar's diabolic drinking-song.

From these instances it would appear that Weber

by preference sought out the extreme sound registers, high as well as low; and indeed he discovered a great many new effects by revealing such characteristic tone-qualities in these opposite extremes. This emphasizing of contrasts accorded well with the nature of Weber's plots. They always hinged on fairy stories or legends with ghosts, good and evil demons, that protected or endangered men and ruled their destinies. The extreme registers of low and high instrumental sound seemed especially suited for suggesting these supernatural apparitions.

Weber knew likewise the capacities of the instruments for expressing idyllic moods. The horn quartet at the beginning of the *Freischütz* overture reveals an entirely new use of the horn's sound qualities in this direction. A significant change had taken place. To Beethoven the horn represented a heroic type of sound and he employed it in this manner in the *Eroica,* in the *Egmont* overture, and on nearly every occasion. In Weber's mind a new association of ideas occurred. To him the tones of the horn symbolized the forest, or—in a wider sense—nature itself. It was the instrument of the hunter, and nobody who hears the opening of the *Freischütz* overture will entertain the least doubt that it is a sylvan mood that is here reflected. This impression may be due to the quartet character of the style, which is so dominant that even the later men's chorus is derived from this horn quartet. Or it may be due to some extent to the

CARL MARIA VON WEBER
With His Conductor's Roll

accentuation of the natural tones of the chord, to which the horns were restricted in those days. At all events, an affinity comes through between the men's chorus and the horn tones, each illustrating the other, both embodying an immediate contact with nature. The same is to be said of the horns in *Euryanthe*. The call of Oberon's horn, again, marches from the beginning of the overture through the whole of *Oberon;* it is so to speak the magic formula, which opens the doors of the fairy world and calls forth all the spirits of the opera.

The extended compass of the winds to include the highest and lowest registers of the flutes, clarinets, and horns especially, the more frequent employment of the trombones for the expression of mysterious moods, the intercession of the horns as symbolic of naturalness or of elemental forces—all these show the tendency of the new romantic orchestra toward animation of the instrumental voices. They receive, beside their function as sounding bodies, a poetic meaning; they become manifestations of a magic world. This principle rooted in the utilization of those organic qualities of the different instruments that were responsible for their colors. The thematic construction of the form was kept, but it supplied only the framework. The distinctive new effect came from the mirages of sound cast by the tonal atmosphere. Tone lost, so to speak, the plastic objectivity of its classic form and was transported to a gleaming incorporeal realm of color; a difference like that between sculpture and painting. The winds of course became the most important representatives of this new principle, but the strings also participated in it. Generally speaking, the mutes were not employed in the classic orchestra, though Gluck used them occasionally, as in Alcestis' way to Hades. Weber made them an important medium for mysterious effects like the apparition of the ghost in *Euryanthe,* quoted in the middle section of the overture, and the intimation of a fairy realm at the beginning of the *Oberon* overture. Weber also augmented the strings, not in number but by the demands he made upon the voices, dividing the first and second violin sections and even the violas into two groups, much as Cherubini made use of a four-voiced cello section. He sought out all degrees of transitional shadings and discovered them in mutable color-mixtures. Yet he also emphasized all effects of radiant brightness, especially in the violins, compositions like the *Freischütz, Euryanthe,* and *Oberon* overtures containing in consequence such verve that they are elevated to virtuoso orchestra pieces, surpassing even Beethoven's overtures in brilliance of effects.

Thus in Weber's orchestra the poetic color element penetrated into the world of instrumental dynamics, marking the amalgamation of romantic conceptions with the former ideal of instrumental language. Unreality, play of fancy, give the key-note and the instruments become the media of an imaginary world.

It is a characteristic fact that Weber, though he also wrote some symphonies and sonatas in his youth, discovered his particular task in the realm of opera. Dramatic action and its atmosphere gave him the stimuli he needed. They enabled him to create an orchestra that included nearly all the potentialities of the romantic tone-language and which therefore has been the acknowledged model for this type of musical performance up to the present. He did not shrink from the final realistic steps in performance to carry out his intentions clearly. In the wild hunt in *Freischütz* he ordered the clanking of chains, the cracking of whips, the tramping and neighing of horses, the barking of dogs. These effects were not only scenic, they were part of the sound requirements, included in and carried along by the orchestra. Within the fundamental assumption of unreality, Weber was absolutely realistic, like his successor Wagner, who from *Lohengrin* up to the ride of the Valkyries showed a special predilection for rendering the gallop of horses in music.

With these naturalistic features the last consequence of the romantic idea is revealed: the exchange of reality for unreality. The conception of the magic world is so overwhelming that all things must be in agreement with it, so that only the dreamed-of idea seems to exist and reality fades to an illusion.

4

THIS was the destined path of opera, and in the discovery of this path the orchestra was the most important, the indispensable guide. But the orchestra on its own account, without the stimulus of the opera, likewise turned away from Beethoven's predominantly dynamic conception. The penetration of instrumental expression by the poetic idea with the consequent revelation of its color qualities extended to orchestral forms as it did to opera, only less obviously. When Schubert wrote his sonatas and his seven symphonies he did not follow the model given by Beethoven either in construction or in point of view. No longer was there a dynamic intent driving toward logical thematic construction and organization of instruments. The structure of the new romantic symphony was softened, the themes were not developed toward a climax. They were to a certain extent revealed by a play of illumination, given by changing harmonies as well as by changing instrumental colors. Harmony itself was interpreted as a medium of color. By delicate shiftings from major to minor or by a sudden sinking of the bass tone a new picture came to life. It was a kind of chromatic modulation which Schubert frequently employed with the effect of sudden translation to a new sphere without other means than surprise.

This was in truth one of his favorite constructive

devices. His themes—those of the unfinished B minor and the great C major symphonies may be taken as examples—are complete at the moment of their first appearance. They are lyric song melodies, far from the forcefulness of symphonic action. They need repetition, not development; but repetition so that an illusion of symphonic action is called forth.

For this purpose Schubert, like Weber, favors the wood-winds, the horns, the mysterious colors of the low trombones, the technical brilliance of the strings. The horns open his C major symphony, the wood-winds, always changing and singing, dominate the slow movements of both the C major and the B minor symphonies. An especially surprising effect opens the Unfinished symphony: the furtive theme in the string basses, the whispering violins, and above them the melancholy singing of alternating wood-winds. All these effects had been previously unknown. It is most astonishing that Schubert should have arrived at them though his practical experience with the orchestra was very slight and he never had an opportunity to hear even his great symphonies. His imagination only had conceived these orchestral sonorities. A certain leaning on the piano is evident, especially in some of the pedal effects in the second movement of the Unfinished symphony, where the strings accompany the singing of the various wood-winds with fading syncopations. The influence of the piano which here asserts itself was not confined to Schubert but became very significant particularly in Schumann's orchestral works. It accorded with the development of piano style itself, which had likewise begun to emphasize color-effects in the treatment of both technique and harmonic construction.

Schubert's use of the orchestra is altogether visionarily conceived. It includes no technical innovations, no instrumental experiments. It depends only upon the wide, almost unlimited, unfolding of lyric harmonies, among which the separate themes, or rather, melodies, carry on a nebulous existence. In a sense Schubert's orchestra, like Weber's, shows a return to a former stage of orchestral functioning. One may even say that it shows also the beginning of a process of dissolution from Beethoven's highly modelled, structurally firm expression of ideas and emotional states to the more vacillating expression of mood and feelings brought about by the shifting color-possibilities of the romantic tone-palette. This process was characteristic for the intellectual attitude of the period as a whole. The inner urge from clarity to obscurity, from daylight to dusk, from plastic objectivity to gradual extinction—this decrescendo line applied in music only as in other fields. The most important works of the composers of the time were written early in their lives. Weber only reached forty, Schubert died at thirty-one, Schumann went out of his mind at forty-four. The decrescendo line is manifest in the inner creative laws of the works themselves, in their order, and even in the personal destinies of their authors.

5

FELIX MENDELSSOHN seems to be the only one who succeeded in striking a certain balance between the great classic foundation and the loosening influence of romantic fantasy. He also ripened early and died young. He wrote his first important work, the overture to *A Midsummer Night's Dream*, in 1826, at the age of 17; he died at 39. He was the only composer of this generation of romanticists who never showed any interest in writing an opera ("music to" a play or story is quite another matter), but from the beginning cultivated instrumental music, for piano and orchestra especially. Not words but poetic moods inspired him, a fact strikingly manifest in the famous title he gave his small piano compositions: "Songs without Words."

His instrumental works in general might similarly be called musical poems without words. They maintained a more precise and objective attitude than Schubert's instrumental works, for example, which may be superior in depth of feeling and wealth of fancy but do not reach such a clear and positive intellectual level. There is a remarkable balance of poetic imagination, romantic gentleness, and formal mastery in Mendelssohn, so that he seems to have been the one authoritative romantic composer who never inclined toward exaggeration of effect or looseness of form. He always adhered to the classic tradition, endowing it with a new poetic understanding of music. He took his inspirations mainly from impressions of landscape, as in "The Hebrides" overture, or from folksongs, as in the Italian and Scottish symphonies, or from legends, as in the overture "to the story of the lovely Melusine," or from poetry as in the overture to *A Midsummer Night's Dream.*

It would not be fair to say that his later compositions were only variations of this last-named, the most famous of his youthful works, or that they represent a less high standard, or that Mendelssohn's genius had exhausted itself with his first great work. But surely this first work encompasses the whole of his creative individuality so clearly that it does indeed represent the essence of his artistic being. Any subsequent compositions might bring greater perfection in particular fields but no increase in essential ability.

In truth it was a new magic sphere that opened with the first notes of this music: with the long tones held by two flutes only—what a surprising beginning! —followed by the second chord with the clarinets added, and so on, until the four introductory harmonies are sounded. Never had such prelude been written for orchestra. It captivated. Even if one came directly from Weber it seemed one of the most original inspirations in sound ever a composer had received. Titania awakes, the whole charm of her elfin

ORCHESTRA OF ROMANTIC ILLUSION

realm is unlocked by these four chords. Now the music leads on simply and naturally, first low and soft, like the hum and whir of invisible dancing sprites, gradually growing more substantial. "Those are gnats, not elves; look at Weber's *Oberon,* there you will discover the fairies" Wagner said. He was not wrong; the difference cannot be denied. But does that prove Mendelssohn's music weaker? Weber was writing an opera, Mendelssohn a symphonic overture. Therefore the more substantial character of Weber's conception, the more sublime nature of Mendelssohn's, sprang from the tasks they had set themselves—apart from the fact that never in any art should a single type be regarded as the only possible representation.

One is always tempted to recall once more the pictures unrolled in this imperishable music, to recognize Duke Theseus and his court, Bottom the weaver and the dancing clowns, to hear Oberon's farewell blessing, which seems to be young Mendelssohn's grateful farewell to Weber, the admired creator of romantic opera. Most admirable of all is Mendelssohn's ability to have ordered all these poetic conceptions in clear and clean instrumental form. Whatever relation they bear to Shakespeare's ideas is reflected not in their structural but in their purely instrumental qualities, through use of orchestral colors. These lie in the wood-wind harmonies of the introduction, and in the divisions and doublings of the string voices with interpolation of chirping pizzicato calls, at the repetition, with the underlying bourdon of the ophicleide and other ghostly voices. It was not the first time that the strings sections had been thus divided. But it was the first time that they had been employed so strikingly for the thematic kernel of a composition, and to this extent they imply an innovation.

But Mendelssohn most rarely used mysterious effects. The transcendental remained outside his conception. He favored soft colors and for this purpose, of course, the importance of the wood-winds and horns increased for him. The remaining music to *A Midsummer Night's Dream,* composed many years after the overture, confirms this tendency especially in the Scherzo with its wood-winds dances and in the Notturno with its melodious horn—again a reminder of Weber's horns as symbols of the forest. There are other striking orchestral effects in the "Hebrides," "Melusine," and "Meeresstille" overtures. Mendelssohn had a particular inclination for the flute, which he frequently employed in a soloistic manner, dominating the wind group. The massed tone of his orchestra shows a certain lightness, caused by the very reserved treatment of the brasses. Mendelssohn did not like the display of force, but favored pastel colors, and it is an exception when, as in the famous Wedding March, the brass group—the very marrow of the orchestra—takes the lead.

All these points attest that while Mendelssohn did

not have the same bold and elemental originality as Weber, he possessed a masterly dexterity and an intimate practical knowledge of all the color values and technical potentialities of the instruments.

That knowledge signifies the difference between Mendelssohn and Schumann. Schumann also had a strong sense of the poetic significance of the instruments, but only in certain very characteristic moments, like the melancholy singing of the oboe or the violins' descending chains of trills in the third movement of the C major symphony. He must have heard in his mind the trumpet-calls for his B-flat symphony and the bubbling flutes in the finale of that work. But Schumann was one of the first of those composers who "orchestrate," that is, sketch the whole work from an abstract sound-idea with certain instrumental episodes and afterwards score it for the orchestra.

Schumann's conceptions were always based upon the piano and his development in the direction of symphonic production was governed by his perception of piano tone. This is just the reverse of Weber, whose piano compositions frequently seem like orchestral sketches, so that Berlioz' orchestration of the "Invitation to the Dance," for instance, appears more original in sound effects than Weber's own piano form. Schumann's ingenuity in transposing piano ideas to the orchestra is often surprising. His works reveal here and there a really original orchestral conception, but by nature he lacked on the whole immediate and instinctive contact with the special characteristics of the orchestra. Nobody could be quicker to hear and recognize them as soon as he saw them in other scores, but to discover and, more especially, to organize them for himself was outside his scope as an individual.

6

THIS primary feeling for organization of the instrumental voices became a factor of steadily increasing importance not only in the conception but also in the performance of orchestral works. We have seen that since Beethoven's time, and owing to the demands made by his compositions, the German orchestras, heretofore fortuitously made up of amateurs and trained musicians, had changed into professional orchestras. But it was not enough to build up the orchestra of instrumental specialists. A guide was needed. So long as the orchestra's main task in performance consisted in uniform reproduction of the rhythms, right entrances, and the correct execution of relatively simple dynamics, the earlier kind of conducting sufficed. Haydn, as we know, conducted in Eisenstadt from the violin desk, in London from the cembalo. With the refinement of dynamic effects, however, and especially with the emphasizing of instrumental colors, the separation of the conductor from the cembalo became inevitable. A personality was needed whose task it would be to specialize in controlling the balance of the dynamics and colors, in defining the more and more complicated rhythms, and in being generally responsible for correct execution in accordance with the composer's instructions.

In this field Weber also set the example. He was the first German opera conductor in the modern sense, conducting no longer from the piano but with a roll of paper. He was not satisfied with marking the tempo, but claimed leadership of the performance as a whole. Thus he created the new type of conductor, who makes himself the centre of the performance. And not only in the reproduction of the music. Weber also made propaganda for the works by public advertisements and explanatory articles in newspapers, by polemics for or against, by efforts to educate the public taste. This appreciation of his task showed a strong pedagogic inclination, which manifested itself in all directions and naturally worked with particular effect in matters pertaining to the orchestra.

The new method of conducting with the baton spread quickly. Spohr reports in his autobiography the astonishment which he caused in England when he conducted with the baton. In reality this innovation was only the natural outcome of the French method, Lully's stamping baton being changed to more manageable form and freed of its pounding noise.

The dictatorship of the orchestral leader in France had created a high state of orchestral discipline and now spread to orchestras in other countries. Mendelssohn, and some years later Wagner, had an opportunity to study the French art of orchestral playing in Paris at the "concerts du Conservatoire," conducted by Habeneck. Now this French tradition was accommodated to the new requirements of Beethoven and of the romantic orchestra. Weber's example in the field of German opera remained, because of his early death, but the initial impulse. Mendelssohn was the first to follow Weber's example and apply it to the concert orchestra.

Through his appointment as conductor of the Gewandhaus concerts in Leipzig, Mendelssohn was able to achieve a far-reaching education of his orchestra, embodying the French discipline in the handling of the new romantic demands. A language of silent gestures had to be invented, gestures indicating not only the entrance of the instruments but more especially the change of tone-color in relation to dynamics, to mutual adaptation, to shaping up the performance so that it seemed truly to reproduce the intentions of the composer. The playing of many men upon many instruments must be made to sound like the tones of a single instrument, played upon by the conductor as the pianist would play his piano or the organist his organ.

In this way a new unity was brought about in the orchestra affecting, as did the earlier unities in turn, not only the composition but also the performance of orchestral works. This was a unity no longer democratic, let alone rational, in constitution, but founded upon and directed by an authoritative will, represented by the conductor. The single players served only as media, all individual qualities disappearing in favor of the one conducting individuality. This was a natural development from the romantic ideology, the first and decisive step in a process which led away from the great spiritual acquisitions of the period of enlightenment into the fantastic magic-ridden realm of romantic art.

Thus, simultaneously with an apparent increase in artistic capabilities we see a fatal loss of intellectual and spiritual independence. The individual instrument yielded up its representative importance, becoming a mechanical component of the orchestra. This orchestra became the reflection of a new culture inspired by a turning away from reality, an absorption in dreams of the past or the unattainable. The tones of this orchestra gave forth the magical mirage of these dreams and the conductor became the magician who conjured these apparitions on behalf of the composer who had caught them in musical form.

VI

The Virtuoso Orchestra of *Berlioz, Meyerbeer, Liszt*

I

While Weber and Mendelssohn in Germany were discovering and cultivating the color qualities of the instruments and creating a new orchestral discipline subject to the authority of the conductor, in France orchestral development was likewise entering a new stage. Since the days of Lully France had had a representative orchestral culture. We have seen how, through the insertion of numerous dances and the emphasizing of dramatic recitatives at the cost of vocal virtuosity, the orchestra had come to participate more importantly in French opera than in Italian opera. Rameau, Gluck, Grétry, Cherubini, Méhul had made use of every stimulus to enlarge the powers of the orchestra. Cherubini had introduced the four-voice violoncello section, and like Méhul he utilized the dramatic crescendo in his overtures. Méhul was especially interested in the horns, increasing their number to four. In his most famous opera, *Joseph in Egypt* (1807), he employed the bass tuba. He liked

THE VIRTUOSO ORCHESTRA

orchestral experiments, writing, for instance, an opera *Uthal* (1806) without violins, taking violas as the leading strings—as Brahms did afterwards in his second Serenade.

The representative French composer of the Napoleonic period was Gasparo Spontini (1774-1851), afterwards engaged as chief conductor in Berlin. He was the perfect successor to Lully. A despotic conductor, he gave his orders no longer with the stamping baton like Lully, nor from the cembalo like Gluck, nor with the magician's baton like Weber and Mendelssohn. Spontini, as Wagner reports, grasped a long baton at its centre and moved it in the manner of a drum major. His orchestra was based upon Gluck's with increased use of the brasses. Spontini introduced the heroic march as a basic opera form heading towards a climax in the triumphal march, an effect still met with in Verdi's *Aïda*. The military character of his orchestra influenced Wagner's *Rienzi*, which was an imitation of Spontini's *Fernando Cortez*, and the first version of the *Flying Dutchman*. But Spontini also refined and emphasized the string effects, frequently using the violas in particular to characterize dark dramatic words.

In the unbroken line of important composers of French opera, Italians and Germans are as numerous as Frenchmen. Gluck was a German, Cherubini, Spontini, Rossini were Italians. Rossini's *Guillaume Tell*, performed in 1829, was one of the most far-reaching successes of French grand opera. Auber's *Muette de Portici* had achieved an exceptional triumph one year earlier and only two years later, in 1831, Giacomo Meyerbeer surpassed them all with his *Robert the Devil*. Meyerbeer was a German. He had studied with Weber's teacher, the Abbé Vogler, a man of small creative talent but with a restless inclination to experiment with sound and with novel ideas. Meyerbeer had first made attempts in the field of Italian opera, turning afterwards to French opera and achieving his decisive success at the age of 40 with *Robert*. Thereafter he remained master of the realm of grand opera. *The Huguenots* (1836), *The Prophet* (1848) confirmed his position, and *l'Africaine*, performed simultaneously with Wagner's *Tristan* in 1865, one year after Meyerbeer's death, may still be found effective to-day.

Meyerbeer's works not only ruled the French opera stage but spread through the whole world because of their musical qualities, their theatrical effects, and the content of their texts. The plots were not limited, like those of Weber's German operas, to a given province of national feeling, but were based upon universal conceptions, especially of historic events of general human interest.

Not only French opera but French symphonic activity also remained on a high level, at first particularly with respect to skill of performance. The "concerts du Conservatoire," which were the continuation of the former "concerts spirituels," cultivated contemporary orchestral works in an outstanding manner. The symphonies of Haydn and Beethoven were systematically practised at the Conservatoire so that these performances came to be looked upon as exemplary. In composition the French were at first less active. An experimentally-minded composer, Lesueur, a kind of musical adventurer, tried to discover new paths by augmenting the instruments and by various other innovations, but without very much success.

2

AMONG his pupils, however, there was one who, suddenly summing up all previous endeavors, and with Beethoven's works as his basis, boldly attempted to create a new type of French symphony. The essential feature of this new kind of symphony was the combination of classic form with a very clear, palpable poetic idea which was now not only woven into the form, as in Beethoven's overtures, but ruled and—wherever necessary—altered that form. It was a descriptive guide, really derived more from opera than from symphony, a kind of compensation for dramatic plot, freed from the accessory details of specific action, restricted to the essential events of the emotional development. The idea of an invisible opera, realizable in the orchestra alone, may be said to have been embodied in this type of symphony which, indeed, represented a new incorporation of the old principle of program music.

This pupil of Lesueur, who surprised and excited the musical world with his first great work, the *Symphonie fantastique*, was Hector Berlioz, originally a student of medicine. Even so clear-sighted a critic as Schumann wrote that on an unprejudiced analysis of the symphony he felt about the same after-effect as Berlioz must have experienced on dissecting the head of a handsome murderer. This happened several years after the publishing of the symphony. Berlioz had composed the work in 1829, one year after Schubert's death, two years after Beethoven's, three years after Weber's, and two years before the first performance of Meyerbeer's *Robert*. The dates show what an abundance of important events in the development of orchestra took place within a period of ten years. During the five years 1821-1826 in which Weber's principal work was done, Beethoven composed his Ninth, Schubert his B minor symphony; in the year of Weber's death Mendelssohn wrote the *Midsummer Night's Dream* overture; two years later Schubert wrote his C major symphony and Berlioz his *Fantastique*; and in 1831, ten years after *Freischütz*, Meyerbeer's *Robert* was performed.

All the forces of orchestral creation seem to have burst forth at once. Fulfillment of the classic orchestra and its mutation into the romantic happened at nearly the same time in Germany and in France. The orchestra, hitherto only one among several elements of musical life, attained within a few years a dominating position, becoming the centre of creative activity in concert as well as in opera and hence in musical life in general.

About twelve years after his *Symphonie fantastique* Berlioz published another work of quite a different nature, the *Traité de l'instrumentation,* a systematic analysis of the organization of the orchestra. Furnished with examples taken from earlier masters, this book gave hints on the use of the instruments and how to increase the range of orchestral effects. Berlioz did not look upon former orchestral types as fixed symbols for given ideals of sound. He saw the changes the orchestra had undergone as a progressive unfolding, tending continuously toward enlargement. So he sketched a utopian scheme of an orchestra consisting of nearly 500 musicians, to be complemented by a chorus of about 400 singers, in all some 900 souls. He endeavored, moreover, to discover new technical and tonal qualities in every instrument and new possibilities for combining them. The contemporary from whom he took the most examples and to whom he always accorded enthusiastic admiration was the German Weber.

In spite of the subsequent publication of several similar works, Berlioz' *Traité de l'instrumentation* has remained the authoritative code of orchestration up to the present. At the time of its publication it was a symptom of the arrival of the orchestra at a new stage: the stage of virtuosity. Virtuosity was at that time characteristic of musical activity in all fields. Its chief representative was the famous violinist Paganini; Chopin was another type of virtuoso; Franz Liszt, stimulated by Paganini, still another. The most famous singers of the time, including the Garcia family—Manuel and his daughters Maria (Mme. Malibran), the first Norma, and Pauline (Mme. Viardot)—the tenor Rubini, the bass Lablache, and many others belonged to this group.

Virtuosity as defined in these artists should not be interpreted in a deprecatory sense; it was no mere exhibition of technical abilities. It was the expression of the unlimited mastery of an instrument in all the finer shades of both its technical and its interpretative qualities. The latter were perhaps more emphasized than the former; the true virtuoso seemed to be rather a magician than an acrobat. The reports of Paganini written by such a severe critic as Schumann show an artist whose most compelling effects were achieved not by his mechanical dexterity but by the demonic fascination of his fantastic improvisations.

Such overwhelming effects could be realized through the violin, the piano, or the voice, the medium in each case being stipulated by the particular individuality of the person whose peculiar visions it reflected. Now the representative of all instruments together, the orchestra, became such an organ of virtuosity, creative individuality being projected into the sphere of orchestral expression through the medium of the poetic program. This program no longer served merely as a stimulus to tone-painting, as it had done before, nor as a sounding-board for the dynamics, as with Beethoven. It became the composer's assistant, giving exact form to his imagination; it became the hearer's assistant, helping him to follow the paths of the composer. Thus it opened but at the same time restricted the field of fancy. A deep-rooted difference between German and French romanticism was revealed at this point. German romanticism strove from reality toward unreality and tried to dissolve all concrete objects in the twilight of poetic moods. French romanticism on the contrary strove after plastic objectivity even in the realm of sound-phantasmagoria.

3

IN HIS *Symphonie fantastique* Berlioz achieved this plastic objectivity through the so-called *idée fixe,* a single melody symbolizing his sweetheart which appears in all the movements, going through continual changes from the ideal object of his longing down to the distorted figure of a witch. In the "Harold" symphony, intended for Paganini as the soloist, it is an instrument, the solo viola, which symbolizes Childe Harold. The "Damnation of Faust" and the "Romeo and Juliet" symphonies are based on well-known dramas and the instrumental pieces are relieved by the insertion of songs. This kind of program music was in truth from the beginning opera in disguise and must in time lead the composer back to opera, as it did Berlioz with *Benvenuto Cellini, Beatrice and Benedict, The Trojans*. The same course of development has in more recent times been followed by Richard Strauss.

Berlioz' program always revealed itself as a dramatic idea. In his *Requiem* he required beside the main orchestra four small orchestras, posted to the North, East, West, South, which were to symbolize the events of the Last Judgment. This arrangement gave a new heightening of effect. The main orchestra, too, shows an astonishing multiplication of instruments: 25 first and 25 second violins, 20 violas, 20 celli, 18 double-basses, 4 flutes, 2 oboes, 2 English horns, 4 clarinets, 12 horns, 8 bassoons, in addition to the four small orchestras consisting of brass instruments and percussion.

The increase in the number of instruments is an important innovation but by no means the only one. In his treatment of the separate instrumental sections Berlioz also showed his inventive spirit and the subtlety of his feeling for sonority. The strings, written now in an unrestricted virtuoso manner are often damped to effects of charming delicacy, as in the waltz of the sylphs in "Faust," when the violins *con sordini* are accompanied by two deep flutes, harmonies

THE VIRTUOSO ORCHESTRA

of the harp making the bass, or in the Allegro of the *"Carnaval romain"* overture, when the secret beginning of the carnival is described by the hastening voices of the strings, or in that singular orchestral cobweb the "Queen Mab" scherzo from the "Romeo and Juliet" symphony.

Berlioz was the first to employ certain virtuoso effects of bow technique in the orchestra, as for example the spring-bow in Mephisto's serenade. He also prescribed the binding of notes in a single bow no longer according to the phrase but for practical performance. He was always inventing new tonal effects. In Margrit's song, "The King of Thule," one viola plays the solo, six others, with flutes, clarinets, and horns, accompany, individual values thus being weighed in the most careful way.

With equal skill he employed brilliant string effects (for instance, in the rustling passages of the overture to *Benvenuto Cellini*), as he had studied them in Weber's music. Brightness and softness, including all transitional degrees, mark Berlioz' string orchestra. He frequently uses expedients to change the sonority: the sordini, the division of the sections, harmonics, soloistic effects. He regularly adds the harp, if possible several harps, as an important help to the strings. It gives a new, glittering, intermediate color. Its occasional use for accompanying thins the atmosphere and at the same time relieves the second violins and violas, which can now be used for other purposes, as in doubling of the melodic line of the first violins.

But Berlioz' main interest belongs to the woodwinds. He does not, like Weber, favor certain ones; all of them—flutes, oboes, clarinets, English horns, bassoons—assume an important position in his orchestra. Their ensemble effects produce that special soft vibrancy and occasional shrillness, which are distinguishing marks of the Berlioz orchestra. Such effects are of course particularly impressive when performed by instruments hitherto seldom used. The English horn, for instance, had been employed neither in the classic nor in the German romantic orchestra. Now through Berlioz it regained the position it had held in the pre-classic orchestra of the 18th century. Berlioz, who benefited by certain improvements wrought by instrument-makers in Paris, made use in unforgettable fashion of the elegiac singing of this instrument, as at the beginning of the *"Carnaval romain,"* when the English horn quotes the melody of the canon-duet, and in Margrit's song in the "Damnation of Faust," when it introduces the melancholy tune *"Ma tranquille."* In one of the most poetic scenes Berlioz ever wrote, the *"scène aux champs"* from the *Symphonie fantastique*, the English horn and oboe, the voices of the two shepherds, first, answer one another, then one disappears and only the English horn is left—symbol of an utter loneliness.

THE VIRTUOSO ORCHESTRA

But Berlioz was also fond of the grotesque effects of the winds and used them especially in demonic scenes, such as the camp of the brigands in "Childe Harold," or Faust's descent into hell or—one of his most original conceptions—in the last movement of the *Fantastique,* when the *idée fixe* appears, distorted to the rhythms of a witch's dance, in the mean tones of the E-flat clarinet, accompanied by the shrill C clarinet and two oboes, while the bassoon provides a galloping bass.

But such striking solo effects aside, the wood-wind group on the whole represents the most important and most influential section of Berlioz' orchestra. Such examples as the *"Menuet des follets"* in "Faust"—an ensemble chiefly of wind alone with an opposing group of strings—laid the foundation for the development of the wood-wind instruments and their players in France, so that the French orchestra has maintained the lead in this art up to the present. The general French conception of orchestral sound may be said to have grown from the increasing importance of the wood-winds and the general German conception from that of the brasses, especially the horns, trumpets, and trombones.

Berlioz also employed the brass group frequently, sometimes with great stress, as in the four small orchestras of the *Requiem.* Aside from the fact, however, that these brass episodes reveal only the more external qualities of his genius, he had not at his command the right instruments to express the natural character of the brasses. Such instruments were a German specialty. The French brasses, lighter and narrower in construction, were with time complicated by valves, which gave greater assurance but diminished the naturalness of the tones. The *cornets à piston* certainly increased the technical fluency of the brass group but reduced its martial sound. The French trumpets, trombones, and especially the horns, were not to be compared with the German instruments of the same type. There are only a few examples of a really elemental effect among Berlioz' brasses, the Racoczy March from the "Damnation" with its overpowering crescendo effects being an exception demonstrating an organic coöperation of all groups.

Thus not only the construction of the wood-winds but the arts of playing and composing for them became a specialty of French music. The strings had now to share their supremacy with the wood-winds. This seems to have been the result of general conditions in the French manner of perceiving sound, originally deriving perhaps from the qualities of the singing voice. At any rate it proved one of the first typically national utterances in the French orchestra, as was the predilection for the brasses in the German orchestra.

Berlioz appeared to be a revolutionary and he was one so far as his orchestral apparatus, the augmentation and utilization of its instruments, was concerned.

THE VIRTUOSO ORCHESTRA

He knew all the subtleties of the sound qualities of each instrument; he knew how to change and to combine the different registers. One might without exaggeration maintain that nothing has since been done with the orchestra that was not done, or at least indicated, by Berlioz. He was master of his orchestra as Paganini was master of his violin and Liszt master of his piano; indeed, he was the perfect virtuoso of the orchestra and it would be difficult to say which came first in his mind, the idea of achieving some effect or the poetic intention that went with it.

But Berlioz revolutionized only the orchestral apparatus itself, and perhaps the musical form in so far as it made use of this apparatus. From a purely musical point of view, with respect to harmonic and thematic development, the revolutionary importance of Berlioz is generally overrated. He did introduce the *idée fixe* into the symphonic organism and with it the uniformity of the main theme and the consequent connection, poetic and musical, between the single movements. This, as we have seen, was not entirely an innovation but carried on a principle already used by Beethoven in his Fifth and Ninth symphonies, also by Weber and other contemporaries in the form of the reminiscence melody.

Taking this principle as a nuclear idea in symphonic construction, Berlioz advanced one step, but only one. He did not dare take the full consequences of creating from the uniformity of the theme the uniformity of the form, as Liszt did in the symphonic poem, or the uniformity of the dramatic development, as Wagner did in opera. Berlioz proved to be, after all, a conservative. He enlarged the form, but he respected its fundamental principles of the several movements and of harmonic development. He was so pedantic in details that he even took Beethoven to task, because in the thunderstorm of the "Pastoral" he had written the cello and the double-bass parts not wholly in agreement, the double-basses in four sixteenths and the cellos in five. This was certainly not correct according to the rules of harmony, but Beethoven did not care for rules in this instance because the effect was correct according to his purpose, which was the portrayal of a thunderstorm. Berlioz' protest against an exceptional instance of harmonic audacity on Beethoven's part afterwards found its counterpart in Wagner's conjecture that the famous clash of the horn's E-flat call with the violin sixteenths B-flat-A-flat, immediately before the repetition in the first movement of the "Eroica," must be a copyist's mistake. Thus both these apparent revolutionaries, Berlioz and Wagner, were more anxious about harmonic correctness than the classicist Beethoven himself.

4

BERLIOZ indeed never wrote a modulation that did not wholly obey the school rules of harmony. Despite

THE VIRTUOSO ORCHESTRA

his most subtle ear for instrumental color, he never dared experiment with the tonal connections in musical design. Considerably more daring in this respect was his contemporary Meyerbeer. Born in 1791, hence twelve years older than Berlioz and six years younger than Weber, Meyerbeer, as we know, had studied in Germany and tried different paths as a composer, his exceptional fame dating only from the performance of *Robert the Devil* in Paris in 1831, two years after the composition of Berlioz' *Fantastique*.

Meyerbeer belongs to that group of artists whose glory has been burdened with moral defamation on the assumption that he aimed at superficial effects—"effects without cause," said Wagner. It has become fashionable to speak of him with a certain disregard, and seems improper to acknowledge other than perhaps certain merely technical qualities of his art. But such moral judgments prove highly untrustworthy, frequently originating in selfish interests or insufficient knowledge of the subject criticized. From the point of view of orchestral development Meyerbeer represents one of the most influential masters of the epoch of virtuosity, while from a purely musical point of view he was one of the most original inventors. His harmonic fantasy, the mainspring of his creative force, far surpassed that of Berlioz. It may be another question to what ends he used these qualities, but an honest answer to that question presupposes absolute freedom from prejudice toward the composer and the conditions of his epoch.

Berlioz esteemed Meyerbeer highly and quoted many examples from his works in the *Traité de l'instrumentation.* As a matter of fact, Meyerbeer employed many of the same effects as Berlioz and it may be difficult to decide in some cases who took precedence. But Meyerbeer had not Berlioz' insatiable desire to augment the orchestral cast. The scores of *Robert, The Huguenots, The Prophet,* show the customary number and kinds of instruments with the addition of English horn, bass-clarinet, occasionally five trombones for special purposes, and ophicleide instead of tuba. In *The Huguenots* the old viola d'amore was employed, but only for a single number. The distinguishing characteristic of Meyerbeer's orchestration is not the abundance of the instruments but his use of them in soloistic and concertante style and in combination with the singing voice. Thus he gained stimuli for the instrumental execution from the singer. In the famous love-duet from *The Huguenots* he bids the cello, which repeats the melody, *"imitez les inflexions du chanteur."*

His ballet music, always an important item in grand opera, shows the immense wealth of Meyerbeer's fantasy in the exploitation of sonorities through soloistic treatment of the instruments. He knew the special effects of the clarinet's deep tones and often combined them with the English horn, low horns, and double-basses. On the whole he knew the poetic effects to be drawn from all shades of tone-color and used them with admirable sureness of touch and without the least importunity.

It is perhaps Meyerbeer's use of keys that manifests the most interesting and distinctive quality of his treatment of the orchestra. He strikingly favors keys with many accidentals, such as B or G-flat or F-sharp. The great duet from *The Huguenots* is written in G-flat major, the famous septet and the prelude from *l'Africaine* in B major, the charming "Paradiso" aria from the same opera in F-sharp major. Wherever we look in his scores we discover this prevalence of the keys with complex signatures. What may be the reason?

It makes no difference to the singer in what key he is singing except as it affects his range. But Meyerbeer may have observed that the wood-winds sound best and that their color, especially that of the oboe, clarinet, and English horn, reveals itself most impressively in the more remote keys. He favored these keys the more because his orchestra, like that of Berlioz, was based upon the sonorities of the wood-winds. But the extreme keys also proved especially suitable for the display of new and peculiar harmonic effects resulting from a more frequent use of the chromatic style, the so-called enharmonic changes. At this point a certain similarity between Meyerbeer and Chopin is to be noted. Chopin likewise preferred the more remote keys, partly because the frequent alternation they required between the black and the white notes on the piano proved advantageous to the exhibition of piano technique, partly because these scales offered more opportunities for chromatic alteration.

Meyerbeer put all his exceptional and original gifts at the service of the opera. He never wrote symphonic works, even his operas containing no overtures, only short preludes. His imagination needed stimulation from the scene, his music was so to speak the sonorous setting for the action. Look where we will in his scores, their descriptive tendency is always their main feature. Meyerbeer is usually condemned for snatching at effects; only the fourth act of *The Huguenots* is acclaimed because Wagner allowed it to be so. But this condemnation is entirely unjust to Meyerbeer's outstanding musicianship and especially to his treatment of the orchestra.

There is for instance that great scene in the fourth act of *The Prophet* in which Jean, having been crowned in the Cathedral, presents himself to the people as the Prophet, the son of God. Just at this moment his mother, Fides, who has been given to understand that her son was murdered by the Prophet, perceives him and cries "My son!" Everybody is astonished, frightened. Could the holy prophet be the son of this poor woman? It is a dangerous situation. If Jean recognizes Fides as his mother he reveals himself as an impostor, if he de-

THE VIRTUOSO ORCHESTRA

nies her, she may be guilty of blasphemy. At this moment Jean has the presence of mind to treat her as insane and to demonstrate to the people the miracle of her healing. He orders his companions to draw their swords against him and to kill him if he has deceived them. And now, apparently exorcising, he asks his mother: "Am I your son?"

The musical interpretation of this exorcism is one of the outstanding orchestral masterpieces of all times. It begins with a lyric cello melody, continued by the bass-clarinet, and these instruments seem to express Jean's love for his mother, his plea to her not to betray him. Then, when he asks, the trombones, low clarinets, and English horn accompany his question with solemn, mysterious harmonies. There is a breathless tension of expectation also as he repeats the question. Everyone looks to Fides, waiting for the miracle. And now suddenly a Lohengrin-moment dawns, the light breaks through: high flutes and violins tremolo are sounding. Fides, trembling for her son's life, understands that she must save him. As if touched by a supernatural illumination she stammers against the shimmering sounds: "No—no—he is not my son!"

This is only one of many episodes which can be discovered in Meyerbeer's scores. They show that Meyerbeer knows the inmost secrets of the instruments, their colors, their harmonic significance, even though he frequently employs these qualities, it is true, as mere sonorous side-scenes and the object they illustrate may seem at times not worthy of the great art expended on it.

5

BERLIOZ, despite his restless instrumental inventiveness, was limited to the basic plane of traditional harmony, and Meyerbeer, despite his ingenious knowledge of orchestral colors and harmonic expressiveness, was limited to the conventional opera. Liszt, the third of this group, surmounted both these barriers. He never wrote an opera, indeed—a youthful work, *Don Sancho,* cannot be included—though he was always very much interested in this species. Perhaps he would have tried to do so, if his friendship with Wagner had not caused him to take other paths. But he had studied very well both Berlioz' and Meyerbeer's scores, Berlioz for his poetic and orchestral tendencies, Meyerbeer for his general musical innovations. What Liszt added to them both was the gift of a new, more highly cultivated and far-sighted comprehension, which permeated the creative principles of his form and of his harmonic construction.

Liszt began as a piano virtuoso. But in spite of his fascinating virtuosity, which made triumphal marches of his European concert tours, he never felt so exclusively bound to his instrument as Chopin did. For Chopin the piano was the only medium of performance, his ideas were stipulated by his instrument and

BERLIOZ
Conducting

(*Gustave Doré*)

LISZT *Conducting*

THE VIRTUOSO ORCHESTRA

he never conceived a motive which could not be perfectly expressed by it. Liszt's sound conception likewise was based upon piano tone, but it was not limited by it. With time Liszt sought a larger frame; the piano conception proved to be only the first sketch of an idea. The vehicle, whatever it might be, that could most impressively convey this idea, was his goal.

A considerable number of Liszt's piano compositions acquired their definite form only when later changed into orchestral clothing, as for instance the Mazeppa étude. Liszt's creative work was always primarily directed by the poetic aim, the instrumental form being secondary, and depending upon the state of his own development and on his growing experience with the most effective kind of musical expression.

His orchestral style consequently did not grow like that of Berlioz and Meyerbeer, from the orchestra, but the orchestra was put to the service of ideal conceptions. It has often been maintained that the orchestration of Liszt's works was done not by himself but by his assistants, mainly by Joachim Raff. In so far as this statement assumes less careful interest on Liszt's part or insufficient knowledge of the instruments, it must be regarded as a malicious insinuation. Yet it may be that Liszt, like many earlier composers, had no scruples about leaving technical details to be carried out by assistants under his supervision, a practice common not only among composers but also among contemporary painters, both of whom emphasized the essential importance of the intellectual conception. From this basic point of view the completion of the work seemed to be in the main a purely technical affair.

From the instrumental point of view Liszt's orchestration does not excel in striking originality. He utilized the achievements of Berlioz and Meyerbeer, indeed, not in an imitative but in a critically selective manner. But he did not increase the orchestral vocabulary by new effects. Not that he did not here and there achieve some original effects, as at the beginning of the second movement of the "Faust" symphony, when the appearance of Gretchen is characterized by the lovely oboe melody, accompanied by the viola's solo. In the "Dante" symphony, again, the four horns and two trumpets convey the inscription above the door of hell: *"Lasciate ogni speranza voi ch' entrate,"* thus answering the preceding declamation by the trombones and tuba of *"per me si va nella citta dolente . . . ,"* the words in both cases being written below the instrumental voices in the score.

But even these examples bespeak primarily the poetic intention which always searches for the most conformable instrumental expression. This tendency is confirmed by Liszt's indications for the execution of his music, such as *"ironico"* or *"con scerno"* (sneering) or *"vacillando,"* and so on, which deviate from the usual musical terms and are engendered by the poetic intent.

Liszt's orchestral compositions consist chiefly of two great symphonies, "Faust" and "Dante," and twelve symphonic poems, beside the oratorios *Christus* and *Saint Elizabeth* and the *Gran Mass*, which are the most important of his ecclesiastical works. These choral compositions show a growing tendency to return to earlier vocal forms, the orchestra being used in a colorful but generally subordinate manner. Liszt's symphonic works are striking not for their instrumental cast, which remains restricted to the orchestral type used by Weber, with addition of the English horn and the bass-clarinet, but for his method of form construction and the development of that harmonic principle, which had already been used by Schubert, Chopin, and Meyerbeer: chromaticism.

Here indeed was a new scheme of colors, arising not out of the instruments themselves but from the refining of the transitions from tonality to tonality. It was a new principle by which sounds were mixed, as it were, by gliding connections. In a way it was the beginning of a process of dissolution of established harmonies. Thus it proved to be a medium for conveying suspended, transitory moods, indefinite emotions, searchings, longings. If Liszt wants to sketch the inflammatory, piercing qualities of Faust's nature he symbolizes them by a sequence of augmented chords, and if he wants to describe Mephisto's negative being he takes the same theme in rhythmic distortion.

Combining of the symphonic movements may have been stimulated by Berlioz, but Liszt's manner of carrying it out shows a stronger compulsion and consequently a more organic unity. He also freed himself from the traditional four-movement form. The "Faust" symphony is built up in three movements: "Faust," "Gretchen," "Mephisto," with the concluding transfiguration; the "Dante" symphony consists of two movements: hell and purgatory, the latter with organic transition to paradise. Both works close with a chorus, analogous to that of Beethoven's Ninth symphony, both avoid fragmentary episodic construction and always keep the musical and conceptual unity.

This unity appears most strikingly in Liszt's symphonic poems. They represent the logical consequence of Berlioz' *ideé fixe*, being constructed upon this one idea as poetic and musical kernel simultaneously, be it Tasso, or Prometheus, or Hamlet, or Hungary, or the principal thought of Schiller's "Ideals" or of Victor Hugo's mountain poem or of Lamartine's philosophical consideration of life as an unbroken sequence of preludes on the one theme given to man at birth. These symphonic poems seem to represent an intermediate type between Beethoven's overtures and Berlioz' programmatic symphonies. They differ from Beethoven's model by stronger accentuation of the poetic element, from Berlioz by greater emphasis upon the musical unity. They testify to the attempt to unify philosophic or poetic works with music by transmutation of the intellectual essence into musical forms. So they represent the culmination of that tendency which strove to make music directly understandable without violating the organic laws of music itself.

6

THIS striving to make music widely comprehensible, and to clarify its meaning in terms of ideas it should convey, must be recognized as the most deeply rooted element of Liszt's musicianship. It made him the first *socialistic* composer, not in a political but in a spiritual, almost a religious sense, a musician whose aim was to proclaim music to all the people and simultaneously to convey all intellectual values in terms of music. Thus he personified the ideal interpreter, first as a piano virtuoso, who by his transcriptions made propaganda for unknown works and composers, afterwards as a composer who interpreted the great ideas of poets and philosophers in his music, revealing by musical means the emotion which seemed to him their most important content.

In this way romanticism reached a height where emotion rose to be the ruling force. Neither Haydn's classic rationalism nor Beethoven's dynamic construction could satisfy the yearning for the mystic sense of a spiritual background. Musical expression had lost the firm consistency of its classic days; it had been softened and dissolved into color, the diffused colors of instruments as well as of harmony. *Feeling had overcome reason.* Everything seemed to be understandable only through sentiment. Music, turned to the expression of sentiment, seemed to be the true interpreter of life's experiences and the world's events. What musical apparatus could be a better medium for such spiritual tendencies than the orchestra with the multiplicity of its sonorities, the wealth of its harmonies, the flexibility of its forms?

Liszt also carried on his comprehensive activity as a conductor, though from quite another standpoint than Mendelssohn. The technical education and leading of the orchestra seemed to him a secondary affair, and, once blamed for not troubling about the entrances of the instruments, he wrote the famous remark: "we are helmsmen, but not oarsmen." He aimed at shaping the phrase as a whole, not the single measures—probably a transference of the same principle which distinguished his piano playing. So he prepared the new type of conductor growing up in his pupil, *Hans von Bülow,* who combined the pedagogic qualities of the Weber-Mendelssohn type and the interpretative qualities of the Liszt type.

Liszt is one of the most stimulating figures in all fields of music, as a pianist, as a composer (if we consider form and harmonic innovations), as a con-

THE VIRTUOSO ORCHESTRA

ductor, even as a writer. Nevertheless a kind of tragic neglect has persecuted him and burdened both his work and the appreciation of his personality up to the present time. In this his destiny has been somewhat similar to Meyerbeer's. Though both men indisputably possessed all the great qualities, a more or less secret resistance is always exerted against admitting as much. It seems to be good form to underrate these two men and their creative importance. No effort to alter the situation is of any avail; Meyerbeer and Liszt seem to be infected with a power of malediction, so that everyone who thinks or speaks of them with admiration runs the risk of losing his own reputation. Meyerbeer is made an inferior and morbid character both as musician and as human being and Liszt is either a charlatan throughout or at least an impotent composer.

It is apparently impossible to change this impression. Yet it rests upon a mass of untrue statements concerning the men themselves and of unjust judgments upon their works, even involving ignorance of the works themselves. One fact may explain the tenacity of this historical falsification: there appeared immediately after Meyerbeer and Liszt, almost simultaneously with them, another composer, who made use of all the fruitbearing achievements of his two immediate predecessors without himself being weakened by such dependence as they had shown upon the spirit of the age, and who was at the same time possessed of such an overwhelming creative force that he rode over all personalities and productions of the preceding epoch and brought forth a new standard and a new set of values. A sudden change was taking place not only in musical but in all intellectual and even spiritual affairs.

This other composer was Richard Wagner, the most important of the German musicians of the 19th century.

VII

The Cosmic Orchestra of *Wagner*

I

Nearly all orchestral composers up to Wagner had themselves been practical instrumentalists. Lully was a violinist, Rameau and Handel were organists, Haydn was a piano teacher and violinist. Most of the others had begun as piano virtuosi: Mozart, Beethoven, Weber, Meyerbeer, Mendelssohn, Liszt, Schumann. Only one, Berlioz, never appeared with any instrument other than the orchestra, and that happened only on certain specific occasions, chiefly when he had to conduct his own compositions. Moreover he was busy as a writer; he and Robert Schumann represent the literary type of composer.

With Richard Wagner a new type came upon the scene: the conductor-composer. Wagner had never practised an instrument, his piano playing was very imperfect so that public performance as a virtuoso never came into question. Other instruments he played even less well. Yet he was obliged to earn his subsistence as a musician. He did not like to teach, he frequently wrote articles about music and the theatre, but not professionally as did Schumann and Berlioz. His ambition was to be a conductor, a longing which had taken root when as a boy he had seen Weber conducting in Dresden. From that time on his secret desire was "to stand there like that and conduct" ("*so dastehen und dirigieren*"). This desire may have had a psychological root in Wagner's own craving to rule a great organism.

From the point of view of the orchestra new consequences followed from the appearance of a conductor-composer. Men like Lully, Gluck, Haydn, Mozart, even Beethoven—who had been organist and violinist as well as pianist—were familiar with the practical handling of the instruments, especially the strings. In the following period, when piano virtuosi were dominant, this practical knowledge was replaced by imagined conceptions of sonority, frequently, however, inspired by the piano. This does not mean that such composers as Weber, Schubert, Liszt were insufficiently acquainted with the qualities of the various other instruments. But without doubt they gained much incentive from the piano, its effects on dynamics, color, and form. Its mechanism underwent important developments from the beginning of the 19th century and the piano had become, so to speak, the composer's experimental instrument. At the piano he sketched the design which was afterwards to be carried out in orchestral colors. So the piano represented the orches-

THE COSMIC ORCHESTRA

tra in miniature, while the orchestra seemed to be the extension and perfect fulfillment of the piano.

The conductor-composer started from other assumptions. His perception of sonority was not influenced by piano effects because he himself had no association—conscious or otherwise—with them. On the other hand, he possessed because of daily experience in the orchestra a close knowledge of all the instruments. He did not play them all as the piano virtuoso played his instrument; but he had the best possible opportunity for studying both their individual qualities and the combinations they offered, and he thus acquired from the first an objective sense of orchestral sonorities, not particularly biased by the peculiarities of any one instrument. Originally the singing voice had been the model for the orchestra, then the organ, the piano, occasionally even the violin. Now the orchestra stood upon its own feet as an independent unit and its player was the composer-conductor. But at what point did his playing start, and toward what goal was it directed?

Instrumental music at the beginning of its development toward independent forms had striven to eliminate language, to replace words by purely instrumental expression in its own abstract forms which were molded by means of dynamics and color. In Wagner's opinion instrumental music, originating in the dance, had unfolded to a certain high degree of cultivation the expression of human feelings; but instrumental music could never by itself achieve absolutely clear representation of emotion. For this it needed the word, to complete, to interpret its meaning. Wagner believed that instrumental music as an independent species had reached its height with Beethoven, that to go beyond would be impossible, as Beethoven himself had shown by calling the word back again in his great last symphony. In Berlioz' and Liszt's compositions Wagner recognized only experiments in emulating linguistic clearness, experiments which could sharpen the orchestra's capacities to an extreme degree, but which could never achieve perfection because the word itself was lacking. Orchestral music by itself had reached its limits and could no longer be continued as an independent art. A new combination of instrumental and verbal language seemed now to be necessary.

This new union, which must be absolute, could be created only by means of the drama. The drama—no longer opera—must be based upon "word-tone-speech" as the unity of vocal and instrumental media. For this word-tone-speech a new grammar must be evolved, the laws of which should be founded upon the unification of linguistic, vocal, and instrumental forms, and fundamental to the statement of these laws was knowledge of the "purely human." Which means that emotion then became the supreme and unique legislator, "wholly instinctive emotionalization" the standard set. Romanticism was at its zenith.

THE COSMIC ORCHESTRA

2

"A NOTE of music, having acquired emotional universality, forms the vehicle or channel of the poetic idea which through it becomes a direct outpouring of feeling." A sequence of such "outpouring of feeling" forms a phrase (its length determined by the breathing) and so constitutes a *melody*, in which individual notes are related in a *horizontal* sequence governed by the rise and fall of accent.

The notes in a melody have also a *vertical* function. The key which is their emotional sphere has two dimensions, melodic breadth and harmonic depth. The "somewhat indefinite" melodic content of horizontal melody receives "full expressive definition" through vertical harmony, which "completely conveys every important crisis" to the senses. Modern music, an art expressing "undefined emotion," has developed from *harmony*, and word-tone melody can alone give it the emotional definition it lacks.

On the other hand, word-tone needs a foundation of harmony if it is to display its emotional content fully. "Only the kind of melody that modern harmonic music makes possible is the melody that the poet needs and that can at once excite and satisfy him." A meeting-place has at last been reached for poet and musician, word-tone melody and harmony, horizontal and vertical musical expression. "The poet has become musician, the musician poet, together they form the complete artist."

In short, Wagner means that there is no longer an independent instrumental music, there is no longer a melodic sung opera—there is only the union of these two in the word-tone-drama, based upon the musical medium of harmony.

The only proper vehicle of harmony is the orchestra. The orchestra is "a materialization of the idea of harmony in action" and in it "the conglomerate members of the vertical chord manifest their common trend in a horizontal direction." Orchestral speech, differing radically from human, oral speech, possesses, as it were, vowels but no consonants. It is therefore purely emotional, and is analogous to the primary sounds of human speech. The different instruments used, however, supply the variety of sound produced in human speech by the introduction of consonants. The instruments may be divided into consonantal groups, graded as finely as, for instance, the sounds P and B, V and F in verbal utterance. Thus a differentiating principle, comparable with that of human language, may be detected and developed in the construction of an orchestra.

Wagner wrote this exposition of his conception of the orchestra, its functions and its relations to language, in 1851, in the booklet "Opera and Drama," after his flight from Dresden. At that time he had already composed all his works up to *Lohen-*

grin, and the *Ring of the Nibelung* was in preparation. It was the moment at which Wagner became clearly conscious of himself, of his personal as well as his artistic aims. He had to think out the reasons for both his personal conflicts and his failures as a composer; had to clarify the inner motives of his social and creative activity; had to account for his entire development leading to this great crisis of his life.

As a composer he had gained sufficient experience to know all the media that he wanted and the changes he must make to use them further. As a man he had gained sufficient power of self-analysis to acknowledge the difficulties resulting from the conflict between his unconditional demands and the opposing opinions of that time. As a conductor he recognized the incompatibility of his theoretical requirements with the practical conditions of reality.

Therefore he found no reason to hide these contradictions; on the contrary, he revealed them as clearly as possible without fear of consequences. Many details in his aesthetic views he himself discarded in later years and on the whole his polemic outbursts should not be taken too literally. But allowing for the influences of the moment, these statements, written in his prime, in his 38th year, give a good picture of Wagner's fundamental ideas, more particularly his views on the nature and main purpose of the orchestra. To put it briefly, Wagner abolished the orchestra's autocracy and its position as an instrument of virtuosity. He joined it to a greater organism and charged it with a new task. He used all the technical acquisitions of the past, no longer for their own sakes, but subordinated to a higher aim symbolized by his idea of drama.

3

FOR Wagner the orchestra is a cosmic sound organism. The germs, the impulses of life are there, enclosed in it, but still unformed, invisible, as emotions only. The orchestra is nature itself in its primitive stage. It has not the capacity for objective melodic speech, because only language can develop the individual melody. The orchestra has certain relations to language, the differences among the instrumental sonorities corresponding to the differences among the consonants. But the instrumental sonorities remain inarticulate, they are not clearly defined. They can be so only by language, therefore the orchestra must always strive for a connection with language. As speaking man is a product of nature so individual melody is a product of harmony. The orchestra is the organ of harmony. Hence the syllogism: orchestra equals harmony, harmony equals nature, orchestra equals nature or—in Wagner's opinion the same thing —cosmos.

Wagner at this time had a liking for comparisons taken from the field of natural sciences; elsewhere he compares the elements of language—vowels, consonants, etc.—with the structure and the circulation of the human body. These comparisons may help to disclose the direction of his opinion. The orchestra indeed seemed to him to reflect an organic life in a stage not yet of rational expression but still of elemental forces to be ruled by and built up in accordance with the principles of harmony. This was a naturalistic interpretation of harmony itself, which strikingly resembled Schopenhauer's aesthetics of music, unknown to Wagner at that time. The lowest tone is the root, the deepest in terms of space, the darkest in terms of color. Upon this fundamental tone harmony is built up vertically, so that the higher tones gain increasing lightness and mobility and a natural organic life unfolds as the tones ascend in harmonic order.

Wagner illustrated this conception of orchestral harmony most impressively in the prelude to *Rheingold*. It consists only of the development of the E-flat major chord. It begins with the deep E-flat of certain double-basses to which, after a time, the bassoons add the deep B-flat, the fifth of E-flat; again after a time the horn begins with the ascending E-flat chord; other horns—eight in all—follow, ascending and descending; again after a time the low strings and certain winds join, the form of the chord loosens by degrees into a livelier movement, first of eighth-notes, afterwards of sixteenths, the violins and the high registers of the wood-winds participate, but always keeping the one E-flat major harmony. Eventually the full orchestra is completed without the least harmonic change or actual melody. Suddenly the curtain opens, we see the bottom of the Rhine, the swimming Rhine-maidens. At this moment—after 136 measures—the harmony changes from E-flat into A-flat and simultaneously the singing of the one Rhine-maiden begins with the first melodic phrase: "Weia, waga, woge du Welle."

One might think that Wagner wrote his explanation of the orchestra's aesthetic task and its relations to language as a commentary on this scene; or, on the other hand, that the idea for this scene was slumbering in his mind as he wrote those sentences. The example in any case most clearly proves the close connection between the two and thus successfully illustrates Wagner's point. What we see and simultaneously hear is the building-up of organic life—the beginnings of which may be imagined as some primal force, perhaps still below the bottom of the Rhine—that slowly, like a process of creation, ascends to higher stages through all registers of the orchestra, to finish its pure harmonic development with the first sung melody and the first, if primitive, words.

The *Rheingold* prelude is one of the clearest examples of Wagner's identification of nature with harmony, harmony with orchestra. To carry out this principle a peculiar orchestral combination was necessary. At first Wagner increased the number of the

THE COSMIC ORCHESTRA

wood-winds to three for each group—three flutes, three oboes, three clarinets, three bassoons—which made it possible for the instruments of a single color group to play the tones of a triad, the tonic, third, and fifth—in other words, to perform an entire chord. Completing the wood-winds by English horn, bass-clarinet, double-bassoon was no innovation, but the addition of these instruments—until that time a kind of extravagance—now became a regular institution. Like Berlioz and Liszt, Wagner also favored the English horn for important soloistic effects. One of the most famous of these is the great solo, where the dying Tristan is listening to the tune of the shepherd, who is waiting for the arrival of Isolda's ship.

But such soloistic effects are exceptions used only for special occasions. In general the wood-winds appear in a harmonic chorus, even in *The Mastersingers*, where Wagner makes a brief return to the two-voiced groups of his former operas. The decisive turn happens in *Lohengrin*. It is the first Wagner opera announcing the primarily harmonic conception by its alternation of descending and ascending harmonies. The themes themselves, especially the musical symbols of the Grail, show a structure, no longer melodic but harmonic, the tragic idea is reflected by the change from A-major (Grail) to A-minor (the question-motive). Close examination shows that all the themes, so far as they have melodic features, consist of divided triads. They represent in reality harmonic complexes, usable in both horizontal melodic line and vertical harmonic units.

4

LOHENGRIN was a work of transition, announcing the new harmonic style but not with absolute conviction. Only the following period of revolution and reflection brought about that clarity of purpose which made possible—after an interruption of several years—the composition of the *Ring*. Now not only were the wood-winds shaped into organs of harmony, the brasses also took on new importance. Wagner added to them a wholly new group, the tubas, an intermediate type between the horns and the heavy brasses. They were constructed similarly to the large bass tuba but in smaller forms and were played with mouth pieces like those of the horns. They appeared as a quartet and were employed only together for special harmonic purposes, as at the beginning of the second scene from *Rheingold* where they bear out the scenic picture of Walhalla.

In contrast, the trombones frequently appear in unison where an effect of elemental force is needed, as, for instance, in the ride of the Valkyries. Wagner's brass group as used in the *Ring* includes at least four horns, occasionally six or eight (four of them interchangeable with the four tubas), three trumpets and bass-trumpet (the latter also an innovation to complete the harmonic independence of the trumpet

THE COSMIC ORCHESTRA

group), three trombones, bass tuba, and the four so-called Nibelungs' tubas—in all four different brass groups, each of them four-voiced, providing, in other words, four choirs which may be employed singly or, for special important purposes, together.

Wagner used this orchestral cast only for the *Ring* series, eliminating the tubas in subsequent works. *The Mastersingers* especially shows a striking simplification both in cast and in use of the instruments. This is not to be explained by any general intention to effect restrictions. Wagner's instrumental cast always depends upon the character of his plot and the style of the work, and upon these factors only. An opera like *The Mastersingers* with its mediaeval subject induced him to use a similarly mediaeval costume for the orchestra—mediaeval, indeed, only in comparison to his other works. The *Ring* operas, on the contrary, directly invaded the field of elemental nature and events, so that they required the largest and the most powerful orchestral sonority. The chromatic style of *Tristan*, again, did not permit the inclusion of instruments which—like the tubas—were constructed chiefly for the purpose of performing vertical harmonies.

The *Parsifal* orchestra, finally, resulted from new practical experiences with the covered orchestra in Bayreuth. The style of this last work demonstrates most clearly Wagner's tendency to build up his orchestra in the three main sections: brasses, wood-winds, strings. But in *Parsifal* direct material sonority is no longer appropriate, especially that of the brasses; Wagner inclines to avoid all profane sound effects, to deprive them of their immediate reality. The brasses accordingly are not over-emphasized, but all three instrumental sections maintain their special fields as set forth in the prelude.

Despite later changes and certain apparent reductions, the brasses from the beginning represent the foundation and the most characteristic part of Wagner's orchestra. *Rienzi,* based upon Spontini's military type of orchestra and inspired by *Fernando Cortez,* requires the great opera orchestra with tuba, besides a large brass band on the stage. The first version of the *Flying Dutchman* is orchestrated with such an excess of brasses, that Wagner even in Zurich reduced them, as he did in his "Faust" overture. He himself remarked that "one sees on such occasions which rawnesses one has slipped off with time." Yet many good musicians because of its wild character like the first orchestration of the *Dutchman* better than the tame later version.

Tannhäuser also, with its dominating horn and trombone sonorities, produces at first hearing the impression of an overwhelming brass group, the use of which is not restricted to climaxes but traverses the whole work, so that the brasses, formerly only taking charge of certain high spots, now rule the entire sound-picture. The same is true of *Lohengrin,* although the lucid atmosphere of this work produces sharp contrasts with the sonorities of the brasses; even the prelude culminates in the mighty dynamic climax of the chorus of trombones which keep their importance up to the prelude to the third act. The brasses are always an absolutely organic part of Wagner's orchestration and furthermore they fix the fundamental sonority, all other instrumental colors depending upon the dynamic weight of the brasses.

Wagner's use of the strings, both in number and in technique, may be traced to this basic fact. It is, so to speak, a new al-fresco technique that he requires of his strings. Weber, even Berlioz, maintain in their string technique a certain relation with the soloistic type of playing, but Wagner consciously turns away from every vestige of soloistic virtuosity. The strings are to him instruments for figuration and effective paraphrasing of the simple brass themes and harmonies. He demands a highly developed technique, but only with regard to fluency of fingers.

The chromatic figures in the *Dutchman* already indicate the direction of his experiments. The famous, often-parodied violin figures of the *Tannhäuser* overture continue this line, which runs through the chord figures from the Fire-Spell, the ride of the Valkyries, and the Rhine-maidens' scene in the *Dusk of the Gods* to the arpeggios in the *Parsifal* prelude. This means that the strings have also become organs of harmony. But because they are homophonic instruments without potentialities for performing harmonies they are obliged to play harmonic paraphrases, triads separated into moving figures, sometimes in scale-form as in *Tannhäuser,* sometimes in broken chords similar to piano figurations.

Of course Wagner also employed other string effects. He especially favored brilliant string runs in unison, such as Weber used, for example before the coda of the *Freischütz* overture, imitating this particular model at a corresponding point in his *Flying Dutchman* overture. In later works he introduced brilliant soloistic violin runs, as after the march in the second act of *Tannhäuser* and immediately before the end when Tannhäuser calls "To Rome!", or in the prelude to *The Mastersingers* and in the last scene when the apprentices run to the dance. Another example of a special violin effect may be found in the third act of *Siegfried,* when Siegfried reaches the solitary scene of Brünnhilde's slumber. A spun-out solo by all the violins, slowly ascending and again descending, illustrates Siegfried's first surprise and sense of oppression aroused by the view of this unfamiliar world.

All these string passages, whether formed of broken harmonies or of a horizontally developed expressive lyric motive, require a large number of players, because the intended effect can be realized only through performance by many instruments. From the composition of the *Ring* on, therefore,

Wagner prescribes the exact number of strings: 16 first and 16 second violins, 12 violas, 12 cellos, 8 double-basses. This string orchestra is necessary both as counterpoise to the winds, especially the brasses, and to obtain from the strings the effect Wagner demanded.

5

WAGNER'S orchestra is organized as a whole, then, on the principle of harmonic display. Harmony is the starting-point of Wagner's creative conception. For him, indeed, harmony includes the idea of action itself. This holds for the poetic as well as the musical substance of Wagner's work which is based upon "harmonic action," each individual creation representing a different symbolic clothing of harmonic events. Wagner's fundamental idea of "redemption," which dominates his operas from the *Flying Dutchman* up to *Parsifal* is the poetic symbolization of the musical cadence: the resolution of different chords into the fundamental harmony. The ways in which this resolution is conceived and carried out vary from work to work, and they are always of both musical and poetic origin. One remembers his remark about his childhood: "In my daydreams I used to have visions in which the keynote, third and fifth used to appear to me in bodily form and reveal their character and significance." These daydreams continued in later years and indeed they indicate the essence of Wagner's creative impulse to deal with harmonic action.

There are two main principles by which harmonic action may be developed: the principle of *diatonic triad action* and the principle of *chromatic action*. Usually the two are mixed, but in varying proportions. Sometimes triad action dominates, as in *Lohengrin*, a most striking example, where it is created chiefly by the motion of the descending and ascending triads, paralleling the idea of the arrival and disappearance of the Knight of the Grail. Chromatic motives are reserved for the hostile figures of Ortrud and Telramund, who try to destroy the purity of the triads, which nevertheless return to their transcendental source. The counterpart of this triad action in *Lohengrin* is the chromatic action of *Tristan*, which symbolizes insatiable, restless passion and changes from harmony to harmony without a definite tonal centre.

Lohengrin and *Tristan* may be extreme examples of the employment of the two elemental principles of harmonic action, but they prove that the triad may by no means be generally taken as symbolic of the good forces and the chroma as symbolic of the evil. Wagner's idea in this connection changes incessantly. In the *Flying Dutchman* the triad motive—consisting of the keynote and fifth only, without the third—represents the unrealizable longing of the damned, and Senta's ballad completes this empty chord with the major third. The chromatic motive paints the turbulence of the ocean and creates the atmosphere which makes credible the stormy events in the souls of the men. In *Tannhäuser* the sacred love of Elizabeth and the profane love of Venus are contrasted by means of the diatonic and chromatic tonal spheres.

The *Ring* continues the contrast of triad action with the opposing chromatic forces of the dark passions. Harmony is now the symbol of elemental nature, which is disturbed and destroyed by rapacity and despotism. In the harmonies of *The Mastersingers*, with their mediaeval flavor, the triad characterizes a well-ordered though restricted world-picture, while in *Parsifal* it becomes the symbol of the highest, the divine community, which is attacked by the inferior passions characterized by sensual chromatic harmonies.

This brief analysis reveals the main principles alone and should be used only in a general sense. But it discloses the creative under-current, manifest in various forms, which is caused by the attempt to balance the contrasts of diatonic and chromatic harmonies. This balance is reached with the final harmonic resolution, in music known as "cadence," in the concepts of poetry called "redemption."

Thus Wagner's dramatic action is conditioned by the phenomenon of harmony. The organ of this harmony is the orchestra, formed in every detail to meet the demands of harmonic expression. For this purpose the wood-wind group is enlarged, the fundamental brass group is augmented, the number and the technical treatment of the strings are altered. All this is done in order to perform complete harmonies, to make them as impressive and as varied as possible in sonority, dynamics, color.

For the same reason which induced Wagner to identify the orchestra with creative nature itself, he also chose for his subjects spheres of dramatic action which bore some relation to nature. He had begun with a historical plot, *Rienzi,* from which he turned in the *Flying Dutchman* to an amalgamation of elemental forces and human feeling, and from this again, with *Tannhäuser,* to a conflict of passions within man himself. But the leaning towards nature increased, it led from *Lohengrin,* with its revelation of secret forces in human nature, to the *Ring of the Nibelungs.* With the conception of the *Ring* Wagner had arrived, so to speak, at the heart of nature itself. There is the Rhine, the thunderstorm with the riding Valkyries, the Fire-Spell, the waving forest in *Siegfried*—pictures taken from nature, which are reflected again in *Parsifal* in the Good-Friday Spell, sketched at this period in Zürich.

Wagner's gradual withdrawal from these naturalistic conceptions may be observed to correspond with the ascent from *Rheingold* to *Walküre* and the first part of *Siegfried.* It continues through Tristan's night of passion and the demoniac enchantment of the Paris

Venusberg to the bright daylight of *The Mastersingers*, to the awakening Brünnhilde of the third act of *Siegfried*, to the masterly conclusion of the *Dusk of the Gods*. The goal is reached with the building of the mystic temple of the Grail.

The orchestra takes part in all these changes. One might even say that it is one of the creative forces which cause them. Appreciation of the orchestra's potentialities, of its abilities to carry out transformations, was one of Wagner's most important artistic qualities. While it might be an exaggeration to maintain that this gift was the supreme element of his genius, there is no doubt that Wagner's creative activity was guided primarily by the force of his instrumental imagination. His orchestra mirrored his scenic visions, and vice versa these scenic visions were called up by the orchestra. One might say that *Wagner heard the scene with the ears of the orchestral composer and saw the orchestra with the eyes of the scenic poet and painter.*

6

WAGNER's peculiar orchestral style, the technique or principle of the so-called *"Leitmotiv,"* reflects a similar process. This Leitmotiv is derived from both the romantic remembrance-motive, especially as Weber and Meyerbeer employed it, and the *idée fixe* as used by Berlioz and Liszt. But Wagner surpassed them all in his logical and consistent use of this principle in the development of a uniform musical organism. His Leitmotiv, as he came in time to employ it, was not only an episodic presentiment or recollection. It was a musical and simultaneously a poetic interpreter of dramatic action. As a poetic medium it was used to carry out a complete psychological process, an uninterrupted chain of conscious and unconscious mental events. As a musical medium it represented the continuation of Haydn's and Beethoven's method of thematic development. The Leitmotiv took the place of the former theme from which the symphonic organism was constructed.

Hence Wagner declared further symphonic production to be superfluous. He believed he had taken over the fruitful principle of the symphony by changing the theme into the Leitmotiv. This he developed toward a new aim: the dramatic-musical action, which was so clear that it did away with the ambiguity of the purely instrumental symphony and did not need explanation in the form of a program. Wagner's Leitmotiv was no longer a thematic individuality in the classic sense but only a harmonic fragment altered into a melodic variation. So his Leitmotiv-technique cannot really be compared, even in its highest manifestations as in *Tristan* and *The Mastersingers*, to the musical compactness and intellectual significance of true symphonic construction.

But the Leitmotiv was the most suitable medium for penetrating and animating the new harmonic or-

THE COSMIC ORCHESTRA

ganism, and at the same time it was a medium for clarifying the emotional progress of the action. Furthermore, it was a familiar device and hence helpful to the mind in following the development of both the musical and the dramatic action. From not only its melodic and rhythmic variability but also its possibilities for sonority resulted an ever-changing emotional significance. The Leitmotiv was, so to speak, the principle of life, the creative formula taken from harmony, returning to harmony, and in this process constructing a complete imaginary system of harmonic action.

To produce this picture perfectly was always one of Wagner's most important tasks. From the time of his practical activity as a conductor in Dresden he was interested in every problem of the orchestra, no matter what it might be: the qualities of the instruments, the living conditions of the musicians, their education or the practical needs arising from their activity. One of the most important points seemed to him to be the question of the right place for the orchestra. We remember that the Belgian composer Grétry (1742-1813), had already touched upon this question, but only from an outside point of view; he was bothered by the desk-lights and by the sight of the blowing and sweating players. To Wagner these were but secondary matters. More important to him was the problem of obtaining the right acoustic effect. He had enlarged the orchestra, not out of a mere desire for loudness, for he was musician enough to see the necessity for a right balance between voice and instruments. But he needed to augment the actual number of instruments, especially of the winds, because of their colors and their harmonic functions. Even where the instruments had to be softened for the effect in question, to have used fewer of them would have weakened the quality of their sonority without necessarily improving the proportionate relation between voice and instruments.

It is said that as a young conductor Wagner, one day in Riga, by chance obliged to wait outside the closed doors of the green-room, suddenly heard the sound of the orchestra much more clearly than ever before, but free from the disturbing robustness of reality. Whether this is true or not, the idea of a concealed orchestra pit occupied him for a long time; it obsessed and pursued him, so that when he was orchestrating the *Ring* and laying the first plans for a special festival-play-house, this idea was already incorporated in his conception. But it was a long way from the first "Sketch for a Festival-Play-House" to the achievement in 1876. But even now when Wagner for the first time heard the sound of this concealed orchestra it amounted to a new experience, because hitherto he had only been able to imagine the effect of the muted orchestra.

On the basis of this new experience he wrote *Parsifal*, the orchestration of which is indeed the manifestation of a final wisdom on the part of one who was both a great composer and a great conductor. Here Wagner's principle of orchestration is revealed in absolute transparency. The orchestra is divided into three choirs: brasses, wood-winds, and strings. Not only the employment of these three choruses shows the terraced order, but their seats in the orchestra pit too are so arranged that the brasses represent the lowest; the wood-winds, the middle; the strings the highest level; the sonority of the winds being already reduced because of its longer ascent. The pit is partly covered with a sort of roof, which takes the last material remnant from the instrumental tone, so that only the color in a cleansed form, characteristic but no longer robust, reaches the hearer.

This was the effect intended by Wagner the composer, though of course elimination of the disturbing sight of the orchestra was a necessity to Wagner the dramatist. It is to be observed, moreover, that this arrangement is without doubt the only correct way of performing the *Ring* and *Parsifal*. The sonorities of the Bayreuth *Parsifal* in particular, with its architectural harmonies, reveals orchestral qualities never before imagined. The effect, indeed, is dearly bought and the insubstantiality of these detached sounds is achieved only at the cost of their natural freshness and force. *Tristan* and *The Mastersingers* are orchestrally far less satisfying as performed in Bayreuth, and this is even more true of the earlier works, *Lohengrin*,

Tannhäuser and *Flying Dutchman*. To transfer the opera-orchestras of other composers, Mozart or Beethoven for example, to an orchestra pit like that of Bayreuth is unthinkable and would be synonymous with destroying their original sound character.

Since Wagner, with few exceptions, nothing has been done that might supersede his Bayreuth example. The older type of visible orchestra, not in the mystic cavity, has remained the norm for opera in general, the few experimental exceptions proving practically and aesthetically unprofitable. That this should be the case, however, in no way detracts from the fact that it is the Bayreuth orchestra which represents the final embodiment, even to the last logical consequence of its form in space, of the romantic harmonic orchestra.

Here harmony as a creative force has proved its power to organize all phases of musical expression. It has identified the orchestra with nature, it has penetrated it with the vital principle of the Leitmotiv and given it the illusion of a symphonic organism, it has even decreed its position in space as symbolic of its essential form. Thus with Wagner a new degree of perfection was reached: the orchestra had become the symbol of the sounding and creating universe.

VIII

The Decadent Orchestra of *Brahms, Bruckner, Mahler*

I

What happened in the development of the symphony following Beethoven seems to confirm Wagner's theory: that pure instrumental music had reached its height with Beethoven and that it could now only exist and grow in connection with the word, and more especially the word as the medium of drama. Some symphonists had followed Beethoven's example, concluding their works with a sung finale, as Liszt did in his "Dante" and "Faust" symphonies. Berlioz had created a type intermediate between symphony and opera in his "Romeo and Juliet" and "Damnation of Faust." In other cases, words were not used within the work itself but were represented nevertheless by poetic commentary in the programs. These diverse forms of a would be independent instrumental music were what Wagner characterized as mere experiments, endeavors to make up for the lack of language. He demanded the frank return to the word and consequently to action as the indispensable foundation of instrumental music. From this basic conviction all his theories grew up.

There need be no argument over the correctness or incorrectness of these theories, since they were after all not results of an absolute perception but an outcome of Wagner's individual talent. Composers like Berlioz or Liszt had decided in favor of only a loose connection with language not through accident or embarrassment but just because they wanted to be unhampered by language and to employ it only where they had to. In principle, wordless instrumental music had proved its capacity to attain the same clearness of expression as music connected with words, to rise even, beyond the naturalistic, to a higher sphere.

Indeed, all the arguments concerning instrumental music and its freedom from or dependence on words remained matters of opinion. In addition to the symphonies with chorus or indicated action or programs other species of instrumental works wholly free from words or programs were still being produced. Beethoven himself had written eight symphonies without words or—if the "Pastorale" is excepted because of its program—seven symphonies without even programs. Could these works have been only first steps toward the Ninth? Other composers, such as Schubert, Mendelssohn, Schumann had continued on these models, and Wagner's view that their works must be superfluous was refuted by the fact of their existence, their popularity and effectiveness. Wagner's condemnation of pure instrumental music was the more easily to be recognized as but an individual theory by the fact that his contemporaries and immediate followers were producing a new offshoot of symphonic music. Chief among these were Brahms (1833-1897), Bruckner (1824-1896), and finally Mahler (1860-1911).

Different as these three may appear to have been in personality and artistic attitude, they have one quality in common which distinguishes them from all preceding composers, namely their dependence upon the works of Beethoven and the masters who followed him. This does not mean that they lacked musical originality, nor is the statement in any way deprecatory. Earlier masters had been likewise obliged to their predecessors. But the symphonists following Wagner were dependent on their predecessors in quite a general cultural sense. Instrumental music from the time of Haydn to Beethoven, Weber, Schubert, Mendelssohn, Berlioz, Meyerbeer, Liszt, Wagner had conquered a realm of its own. It had developed its own language, partly along purely instrumental lines, partly, in opera or in program music by the assistance of words and action. It had thus created its own vocabulary. Types of expression had crystallized out, conventions of instrumental language had been established, founded upon fixed symbols. Such symbols manifested themselves as forms, as instrumental terms, as principles of development, as methods of technical treatment—altogether as the media of each kind of orchestral performance.

It had been the task of preceding generations to discover these principles, methods, and types and to fix them into symbols, a task that had been solved in most various ways, embracing the most extreme contrasts, from Haydn to Wagner, from Beethoven to Berlioz, from Schubert to Meyerbeer, from Weber and Mendelssohn to Liszt. All these composers had been explorers in the world of orchestra, each had discovered either a new continent or at least a new country or landscape.

Now this period of innovations and discoveries was finished and the period of elaboration followed. The new generation of symphonists took over the complete material delivered to them. This generation had no longer to make inventions, it had to choose among existing possibilities. The forward-driving impulse stagnated; Wagner, the great turning-point, represented the last spur of instrumental elevation. From here one now looked back, surveyed the travelled path, examined the acquired stock, considered the possibilities of further organization. Perhaps this method could be called eclecticism and indeed that is what it was; but only to the extent that eclecticism is the natural destiny of all posthumous generations.

THE DECADENT ORCHESTRA

2

NONE of the three composers who are the main representatives of this decadent period ever wrote or tried to write an opera. Bruckner and Mahler were symphonists entirely. Their other compositions are either studies for symphonies or occasional works and not comparable to the symphonies. Brahms indeed began pretty late to compose for orchestra, only after he had cultivated nearly all types of piano, chamber, and vocal music. Brahms wrote four symphonies, the first of which was published in 1877, when he was already about 44 years old. Beside these symphonies he wrote variations on a theme by Haydn and several overtures. Two concertos for piano and orchestra, the violin concerto, and the double concerto for violin and cello, must be listed among the orchestral works; the orchestral parts of the great choral works, such as the *German Requiem*, the *Song of Fate*, and some others, however, remain subordinate to the chorus. Brahms's first experiments with orchestral composition were the two serenades published in 1860, one year before the first concerto for piano and orchestra.

It has often been said that Brahms's reserve with regard to his symphonic writing, arose from his modesty before the great models of Beethoven. But why should this modesty manifest itself more particularly in the symphonic field and why should the activity in other fields of composition be regarded as less pretentious than the symphony? Furthermore it is absurd to confuse matters of artistic development with points of good behavior. Brahms was not in the least so absurdly modest. If he did not compose symphonies before his fortieth year, the only reason was that he did not feel the need to do so, which means that the orchestra was a medium he did not want. This statement is the more convincing as the style of Brahms's symphonies grew out of chamber music and changed into symphonic style only in accordance with the increasing need for an enlargement in the forms of chamber music.

Brahms was a pianist. But in spite of the fact that he often—especially in earlier years—played in concerts, he never was a virtuoso like Weber, Mendelssohn, or Liszt. For him the piano was no longer an instrument for the display of virtuosity. It was an instrument either for intimate musical expression in the form of a monologue or—in connection with a few other instruments—for chamber music. Both cases reflected the tendency toward a restriction of the size of the audience, a turning-away from the great symphonic community, the change from an outgoing impulse toward the inner life. There was, so to speak, an anti-dynamic inclination. The symphonic platform remained, but Brahms felt no call to orate from it.

His ideal, arising from artistic and personal reasons, lay in an exchange of thoughts from individual

THE DECADENT ORCHESTRA

to individual, the right receptive resonance for which could be found only in a small circle of like-minded friends. This was a new ideal of intellectual community corresponding to the individualistic trend of civic culture. In former times chamber music had always striven towards expansion, until by degrees the orchestra developed. Now a retrograde motion set in, the orchestra was put aside, the volume of sound, the number of instruments shrank.

Brahms, like Wagner, clung to Beethoven's method of thematic development, but in a manner wholly different from that of Wagner. For Wagner, as we have seen, the construction of the musical organism was conditioned by harmonic development; and his Leitmotiv-technique was only a medium for moving and combining harmonies, providing a sort of pseudo-thematic make-up, the themes and motives being in reality split harmonics the development of which culminated in reunion at the cadence. Brahms likewise constructed his form in accordance with a harmonic ground-plan and the tendencies of harmonic development; but his thematic development was not restricted to purely harmonic uses. Starting from Beethoven's variation-technique, Brahms's technique of composition reflected an intellectual process which drew upon models of musical thought preceding Beethoven, particularly the contrapuntal style of Bach's period. Beethoven himself had done the same thing in his last years. This contrapuntal style did not have harmony as its leading element, but developed the thematic individuality of the single voices independently and in relation to one another.

Accordingly harmony now frequently appeared only as the result—intentional, of course, and not merely accidental—of the sounding-together of the voices. This was a very different treatment of harmony from that which preceded it; in fact it indicated not only a reversion but even a tendency towards the dissolution of harmony. Harmony as a compact totality no longer remained the dominating factor; it was not replaced by but combined with harmony formed by several apparently independent voices. The use of chromatics by Liszt and Wagner, culminating in Wagner's *Tristan,* was a similar symptom; but here the chromatic element still remained subordinate to the harmonic construction and could present only a loosening of the harmonic organism. Brahms kept the diatonic order but through it wove the independent courses of the single voices.

Such a principle necessarily led the composer far from preoccupation with the orchestra. For its ideal contrasted with the fundamental idea of the orchestra as a collective instrumental organism; it did not stimulate the utilization of instrumental colors or even of instrumental dynamics. Brahms the musician, on the other hand, was too deeply rooted in the harmonic conception of music to pursue a polyphonic instrumental style to its logical consequences. Indeed,

BRAHMS

THE DECADENT ORCHESTRA

he had no intention of so doing. His musicianship was governed by his striving after a clear and independent expression of his subjective individuality, and the method best suited to himself he discovered in this mixture of elements of a genuine contrapuntal style with those of a conception fundamentally harmonic.

3

THUS it was Brahms who set the first great example of the retrospective attitude in music of the second half of the 19th century. The demand for instrumental color, which had brought about the augmentation of the instrumental groups was put aside, likewise the demand for harmonic color which had induced increased utilization of the chroma. The general principles of form construction, especially of variation technique, showed a regression to Beethoven; the penetration of harmony with the elements of the contrapuntal polyphonic style showed a regression towards Bach.

In his orchestral cast, then, Brahms renounced nearly all the progress and increases made since the time of Beethoven. He employed the wood-winds only in pairs: flutes with piccolo, oboes, clarinets, bassoons with double-bassoons. There is no English horn, no bass-clarinet. All the instruments which had been added with special regard to their color values were eliminated. The brasses also were employed only as Beethoven demanded them in his later works: four horns, two trumpets, three trombones. Brahms added in the Second symphony the tuba only, nothing else. There is no prescribed number for the strings and also the manner of their treatment corresponds to the style of the later Beethoven. This is also true of the treatment of the wood-winds, among which the clarinet is favored especially.

The construction of Brahms's orchestra on the whole, apparently so reactionary, should however be regarded neither as a protest against the Wagner orchestra nor as indicative of insufficient experience on Brahms's part with the modern orchestra. He chose his orchestral cast as he needed it. Indeed he would hardly have known what to do with a larger and more colorful apparatus. He neither took the orchestra for granted nor even found it an especially interesting form of expression. It was only a medium in which to work out his conception, and this conception was based upon a linear, not a coloristic sound-perception.

Brahms's orchestration has frequently been accused of sounding dry or dull or even bad, as if Brahms himself had been unable to achieve a well-sounding orchestration. This is a ridiculous reproach against a composer who already in his First symphony had written such admirable instrumental episodes as the almost transcendental solos of the oboe and first violin in the Adagio or the radiant horn solo in the fourth movement. Criticisms showing such ignorance on the part of the critics concerning the orchestra were

THE DECADENT ORCHESTRA

made for the most part years ago and dwindled as soon as conductors had learned how to interpret Brahms's works and the orchestras how to play them —in other words, as soon as the special nature of Brahms's instrumental style had been acknowledged, that dual style with its mixture of Beethovenesque dynamics and the contrapuntal divisions of the voices, the thoughtful weaving of the motives in a musical web of ever more refined workmanship. While the creative principle behind this method went unrecognized and all orchestral works were valued only for their coloristic qualities, Brahms's orchestra appeared monotonous and pale. But with time the true character and the organic necessity of this new orchestral style were discovered, and then appreciation of the musical design and the importance of strong lines increased.

Brahms's own orchestral style shows a significant development, especially his symphonies. The First symphony, like the First Piano Concerto, reflects the immediate influence of Beethoven's dynamic form construction, even to the tonalities. The change from C minor to C major, the passionate character of the emotion, the progress from a dark and turbulent mood toward a triumphal end—this whole development is typical of the dynamic conception. Hans von Bülow called this work the "Tenth," indicating its relationship to Beethoven. But he added that this "Tenth" was not at all the continuation of Beethoven's Ninth, but belonged between his Second and Third symphonies, a suggestion which places the work very fairly.

In the following symphonies Brahms leaned less and less on Beethoven. The chamber-music foundation of his musicianship became more evident and influenced the character of the themes and their development. Certain passages, indeed, especially the middle movements of both the Second and the Third symphonies, are practically soloistic chamber music enlarged to symphonic form. They represent an unusual symphonic type both in their reflective moods, melancholy or tender or even gracefully playful, and in their instrumental effects, with solo passages for cellos or other strings or wood-winds. This is the Allegretto-type, hitherto unknown in the symphony, foreshadowed perhaps by Schumann. Through Brahms it became a new element in the symphony, much as Beethoven's scherzo had been an innovation in the days of the minuet.

Not only the middle movements but the first and last movements as well gradually underwent a change. Brahms's themes lose the short epigrammatic quality that resulted from Beethoven's clear-cut monumental building, and—as, for example, the main themes in the first movements of the Second, Third, and Fourth symphonies—take on a more songlike expansion. His orchestral setting becomes more transcendent. His dynamic course does not run as straight as Beethoven's. It forsakes the simple and impressive schemes suited to the fresco-effects of the classic symphony; it is full of interruptions, sudden changes; it swings quickly between contrasts, mixing them so that the diverse orchestral groups show diverse dynamic gradations.

Such inner enlivenment of the symphonic organism assumed changes in orchestral style. While apparently keeping to the classic model, Brahms's orchestral style approached the chamber-music type. The instruments had to be treated in an incomparably more sensitive manner, the execution required a greater independence of the individual players. The increased rhythmic complication of Brahms's style, his use of syncopation, and particularly his inclination to mix duple and triple time and to disregard the bar-line in his melodic phrase, demanded, in order to achieve clarity, a soloistic weighing of rhythms and dynamics.

Thus, though in the final analysis a decadent, Brahms was sufficiently original to create a special type of orchestra. His last symphony, the Fourth, summarizes his method and its results. This symphony is the most independent orchestral composition Brahms ever wrote and to a certain extent the highpoint of all his creative work. It no longer bears the least similarity to the Beethoven type, as the First symphony does. Even the key, E minor, is one of the least usual for symphonies. The four movements are built up respectively in sonata-form, song-form (ballad), a scherzo-rondo of triumphal-march character, and *ciaconna*, the old and solid variation-form, on an eight-bar theme.

The epic-lyric character of this work in contrast to Beethoven's immediately dramatic character is evident; the narrative type had replaced the action type. The first movement is based upon the melancholy string-theme and culminates with a canon stretto between strings and winds. The ballad of the second movement with its archaic harmonies gives an opportunity for the soloistic display of the horns and the strings, mingled with mysterious pizzicato echoes, and closes after one of the most beautiful clarinet solos in the whole symphonic literature. The third movement, ostensibly inspired by Thorwaldsen's "Alexander's March" sculpture, brings compact crowd-effects and a dynamic outburst of demoniacal force. Finally the ciaconna reveals in its variations as it were the complete aesthetics of Brahms's orchestration, in both its ensemble and its solo effects. Almost every group of winds has a special variation to uncover its particular sonorities and these all prove to be the same as they were known in the preceding epoch. The trombones are the organ of a special solemn, mystic mood; flutes, oboes, clarinets exhibit their expressive singing. The poetic character of each instrument is that which has with time become the conventional symbol. There is nothing that can be called new in principle, yet everything reveals the genuineness of its foundation. This Fourth symphony is, so to speak, the last word on the classic orchestra as a cultural type and on the Brahms orchestra as a posthumous echo of this classic model.

4

BRAHMS has frequently been called the successor of Beethoven, and this is true enough inasmuch as he used the same media and methods as Beethoven. Also he took over Beethoven's idea of a musical action as founded upon the organic development of the musical elements. Moreover Brahms's art—especially his perfecting of variation-style, his outstanding mastery of all the details of organic musical construction, his seriousness and conciseness of style—surpasses that of all the intermediate composers between Beethoven and himself and justifies the finding of a certain relationship to Beethoven.

Yet it is no more adequate to describe Brahms as the successor of Beethoven than it is to designate any one branch of a tree as the successor of the main trunk. Beethoven, from whom the entire music of the 19th century grew up, had many branches, each of them developing a specialized part of the force of the original, none of them comparable even approximately to the main stem, which includes them all. Within the world-wide range of Beethoven's domain Brahms cultivated but one province, and in it his orchestral work reflects, reduced though it is in extent, an imposing prototype, never to be equalled by anyone again, much less repeated or carried on.

This is true of all composers who have been acclaimed by their adherents as Beethoven's successors. One of these, Anton Bruckner, an Austrian, was born in 1824, nine years before Brahms. Like Brahms, Bruckner composed his first symphony only when he was already 40 years old. But Bruckner began late for other reasons than Brahms. Bruckner developed slowly, and his personal peculiarities were responsible for a considerable part of the antagonism he aroused. Bruckner was declared to be a man without intellect, who had love affairs of a ridiculous sort, who was entirely too absurd to be taken seriously. Even those benevolent judges who regarded Bruckner as a seer standing outside his time, were merely paraphrasing the idea "a man of genius but an idiot." The stumbling-block always remained that Bruckner was not a well-bred man in the 19th-century sense. He was a peasant. This singular fact, whether cautiously avoided or boldly emphasized, caused scandal. Nobody admitted that Bruckner's want of refinement was not a short-coming, graciously to be hushed up, but the very condition which gave rise to the individual characteristics of his creative work.

This admission is needed, rather than superfluous statements to the effect that Bruckner's symphonies contain some nice episodes. The appreciation of these

THE DECADENT ORCHESTRA

so-called "nice episodes" often enough reveals misunderstanding. People imagine they have discovered analogies which in reality do not belong to the essence of Bruckner's art, effects that at best are accidental side-effects. Bruckner's oddness always remains disturbing: his naïveté in contrast with the highly developed intellectuality of Brahms, the simplicity of his structures with their terraced progress in contrast with Brahms's logical continuity, his almost limitlessly flowing breadth in contrast with Brahms's compact solidity, and finally the eventlessness of his music, giving no room to confessions, which in the case of Brahms belong to the organic quality of his music.

These points are not to be denied nor extenuated, nor should they be extolled as signs of superiority. It is only necessary to acknowledge them as manifestations of a perfectly legitimate if somewhat peculiar character. Their legitimacy lies in the evolution of harmony in the second half of the 19th century.

Several paths were open for harmonic development. Brahms had taken one, the path with the lyric, intellectual, cultured trend towards the chamber-music type, the further refinement and specialization of the spiritual element in Beethoven's music. The guide along this way was the ramification of motives. Another path led in an opposite direction, towards far-reaching harmonic complexes to be used as active units. The centre of creative gravity sinks into the depths beyond intellectual consciousness, and from these depths there form and ascend no longer thematic individualities but these sounding unities, moving from harmonic centres of support. The attraction of these centres toward one another, the awareness of only this super-individual process, produces an elemental impression, calls for broadness of form, for apparently episodic construction, the avoidance of thematic detail. Harmony as a complex whole, hitherto only a medium, gains self-importance and itself becomes the initial force.

This was no other than the Wagnerian creative point of view, transported from the field of opera to the field of symphony, freed from all restrictions of action and language—that is, from external formal controls—and left only to the elemental forces of musical evolution. Wagner's "harmonic action," linked presumably with the laws of drama and language, appeared with Bruckner in an independent symphonic form entirely divorced from poetic or programmatic influences. More exactly speaking the great principles of harmonic action, discovered and brought to fruition by Wagner, had by now crystallized into conventional formulas, and these formulas had become symbols for Bruckner's musical language in quite the same way as Beethoven's symphonic and thematic development had provided symbols for Brahms. These symbols of harmonic action had grown strong with time and began a new independent existence in the symphonic organism.

5

BRUCKNER wrote nine symphonies, besides some that are not listed, and his other compositions—a Te Deum, a string quintet, several masses and choruses—centre around this main body of his work. At first these symphonies seem to reflect the fundamental principles and even the melodic types of Wagner's music. But they cannot be regarded as mere imitations of Wagner's musical language, any more than Brahms's symphonies can be regarded as imitations of Beethoven's. Yet the creative principles are the same. Bruckner's themes, like Wagner's, are shaped from dissected harmonies, and his forms, frequently misunderstood because of erroneous comparison with the classic symphony, are based chiefly upon the structural development and eventual balance of these harmonies.

In their vertical order these harmonies represent the natural totalities of Wagner's harmonic cosmos; in their horizontal order they appear to be thematic or even melodic figures grown out of the general harmonic subsoil and with time returning and dissolving into it. Mingled with them are reminiscences of Austrian folk-music. Popular dances in particular are woven into the scherzi. With their original rhythms, these scherzi—which Bruckner came to use as second movements, following Beethoven's model in the Ninth—are the most strikingly effective movements of Bruckner's symphonies, while the great breadth and monumental, even grandiose solemnity of his symphonic style best reveals itself in the slow movements. A significant difference between Bruckner and Brahms is apparent in the fact that Brahms in his Third and Fourth symphonies avoided the Adagio type and he never wrote a regular symphonic scherzo. Bruckner's opening movements, on the other hand, and even more his finales, reveal the inner weakness of a symphonic art based only upon emotional waves of harmony ungoverned by any force of reason.

Bruckner's orchestration results from his attitude as a symphonist. It is purely Wagnerian. Not only because it includes the Wagner tubas in the later symphonies, but mainly because of its whole make-up. It is the harmony orchestra, so organized as most impressively to convey the fundamental harmonic idea of the work. The ground-color is given by the brasses, which occasionally rise to leading importance, as in the Fifth symphony, when a special brass-group is used to blow one theme (a cantus firmus) in a great double fugue—a fugue which moreover strikingly proves the anti-polyphonic style of this purely harmonic counterpoint.

Bruckner's dependence on Wagner has been emphasized the more because of certain changes made by overzealous pupils in his scores. Such conductors as Löwe and Schalk thought to help Bruckner by adding instrumental voices he never wrote or by making cuts and other alterations. Of course these changes, only discovered in recent years, cannot be acknowledged as authoritative, and the truth is that Bruckner's orchestration—as far as it can be reconstructed—does not sound as dependent on Wagner as one has been led to believe on hearing it hitherto. The original on the whole seems to be simpler, more modest and objective, less theatrical than the later versions. But in spite of these differences between the natural and the embellished Bruckner, the fundamental character of his orchestration remains the same, in consequence of Bruckner's purely harmonic style of composition. For the same reason the instruments are treated and interchanged not individualistically but in choral style. The brasses represent the foundation, the wood-winds the second level, the strings the highest.

Bruckner achieves many outstanding and original effects. There is, for instance, the horn solo at the beginning of the Fourth symphony, accompanied by a soft, glimmering string tremolo; and the remarkable slow movement in the same work, a melancholy cello-song, afterwards changing to the violas, accompanied by pizzicati of the other strings. Bruckner has a special predilection for tremoli and pizzicati, likewise for the noble singing of the cello, as in the opening theme of the Seventh symphony. He also frequently uses pedal effects as background of a widespun melody, as in the Adagio of the Eighth symphony.

But he also utilizes all the natural effects of the instruments, especially the trumpet and horn fanfares. The harmonic fullness to satiation, of Bruckner's orchestra, its stirring and radiant sonority, its inexhaustible climaxes, seem to burst through all usual restrictions and to strive after the infinite. Bruckner belongs in fact among the mystics, and his fundamental state of being is ecstasy. Therefore his music is of an ecstatic solemnity and the model for his orchestra is in reality the organ, enlarged to an immense wealth of sounding voices.

6

BRUCKNER was an organist, the first since the time of Bach, Handel, and Rameau who reached the heights of his composer's style from the organ as a starting-point. Brahms had been a pianist. The third of this group of decadent symphonists, Gustav Mahler, was a conductor. Mahler has had to fight harder than Bruckner, even today, for recognition as a composer and against misunderstanding. His symphonies, also nine in number, grew up from the song—not the literary poem but the folk-song, and more particularly that of Bohemian descent. Like Bruckner, Mahler built his symphonies upon not thematic but harmonic

THE DECADENT ORCHESTRA

development. But Mahler, though a pupil of Bruckner, did not draw upon Wagner. He allied himself rather with Schubert and his horizontal or, as it were, level harmonic development. Straightforward, simple singing, in an emotional dream-world of sonority, with a pantheistic background and remote from all connotations of human refinement and culture, such was the ideal of Mahler's symphonic art.

In their musical material and its working-out these symphonies exhibit a striking social, even a socialistic tendency. They strive for effects of unlimited breadth, their dynamic display wants a large compass and a great audience. They are done in the boldest fresco style ever known in symphonic music. In a way they represent popular meetings, gathered around popular ideas which are elaborated in a skillful but nevertheless clear and readily comprehensible manner, so intelligible, indeed, that the highly educated audiences of the 19th century became suspicious, thinking that such clear and easily understandable music could not be good music.

In contrast with Bruckner, who like Brahms always adhered to the purely instrumental symphony, Mahler frequently introduced human voices into his symphonies. There are solo voices which sing songs, there are choruses of mixed voices or of boys' voices only. Occasionally he built songs into his orchestral movements, as in the First, Second and Third symphonies. The first four symphonies indeed are based upon the songs from the old popular collection, "Des Knaben Wunderhorn." In his later symphonies Mahler harks back to his own songs on texts of Rückert; in one instance, the "Song of the Earth," he set Chinese poems, while the Eighth symphony, his greatest work, includes the hymn "Veni creator spiritus" and the final scene from Goethe's "Faust."

Mahler rejected the classic symphonic scheme of four movements. He increased the number of the movements to five or six, or he restricted it—in the Eighth symphony—to two. Only his First, Fourth, Sixth and Ninth symphonies have four movements. In general he wrote no programs, but the poetic idea follows inevitably either from the words of the songs involved, or from the inner spirit of the works.

These symphonies always culminate in the finale. The organic importance of this movement had changed with time. In Haydn's period it had been a light conclusion, in Beethoven's works it stood as a counterpart to the first movement, less important but more brilliant. In Brahms's symphonies its function was about the same, whereas Bruckner's works culminated in the Adagio. For Mahler the finale became the goal of the work. It could be a great dynamic climax, as in the First symphony and the Second (the "Resurrection") symphony, or it could be of transcendental mood as in the Third, Fourth and Ninth, or it could be a full explanation, as in

THE DECADENT ORCHESTRA

the Fifth and Seventh. There were many paths to this goal but they all led in the same direction: toward the finale as the closing collective survey of the whole work. Thus the idea of an inner dynamic construction found its perfection in Mahler's symphonies. This dynamic course was no longer synonymous with action toward a highest point of force. Frequently, indeed mostly, it spent its climax in soft moods as representative of an uttermost culmination.

In his treatment of the orchestra Mahler appeared to be the fulfillment of Berlioz. Like Berlioz he was possessed by an insatiable impulse towards augmentation of the orchestra, an impulse which accorded with the social enlargement of the audience. Mahler augmented the percussion instruments in particular with all kinds of varieties, from tinkling bells and rotas and the xylophone to the great hammer in the Sixth symphony. But though his orchestra included all kinds of brasses, these do not form the basis of the Mahler orchestra as they did of the Wagner and Bruckner orchestras. Mahler's brasses emphasize, accentuate, support climaxes. Occasionally they have solo recitatives, as the trombone, symbol of the voice of elemental nature, in the Third symphony, or the key-bugle (employed for the first time), which plays the main theme in the opening movement of the Seventh symphony.

But in general the brasses are not dominant. Woodwinds, horns, and strings in particular give the prevailing color. There are the gliding and softly singing effects of Bohemian violins, and the oboes, clarinets, and flutes frequently sound more like a small village orchestra than like a great symphony. The break down of the tones, the simple intoning of popular melodies, the increasing predilection for primitive march movements and similar effects, does not require a very skillful technique. But the proper performance of these wood-cut effects requires a simplicity that seems almost too rustic and that at first provokes astonishment and incredulity.

The finest parts of Mahler's symphonies are the middle movements, especially those from his later works, such as the two "Night-Music" movements and the Scherzo from the Seventh symphony or the ghostly and demoniacal visions from the Sixth and Ninth symphonies. In these and other parts of Mahler's orchestral music the whole spell of the earlier romanticists from Weber, Schubert, Berlioz, Mendelssohn and especially Schumann comes to life again; one might say that Mahler in his orchestration has done the things that Schumann wanted to do. The magic of the horn-calls, the charm of the clarinets, of the whispering violins and murmuring flutes, returns again in this orchestra. It is the last echo of romantic sound-symbols, as Bruckner's orchestra was the echo of Wagner's and Brahms's orchestra the echo of Beethoven's.

Brahms, Bruckner, and Mahler, then, are all three

THE DECADENT ORCHESTRA

reminiscent of a preceding period of original creation. Yet they all produced original works each in his own distinctive manner. With these three great composers the development of the orchestra, of the symphony at least, seems to have reached a furthest point. Some other creative stimulus had now to be introduced to produce new contributions to instrumental and orchestral evolution.

IX

The National Orchestra of *Verdi, Bizet, Smetana, Tschaikovsky, Sibelius*

I

THE Brahms-Bruckner-Mahler group represents for the first time a distinctively German type of symphonist. This is true both in the quality of thought behind their music and in the treatment and the sonority of their orchestras. The treatment showed those characteristics which from the time of Weber had become the ear-marks of the German orchestra: construction upon the basis of the brasses, special attention to the horns and clarinets, the arrangement of harmony in such a way that each group—strings, wood-winds, brasses—started out as harmonically self-sufficient, combinations appearing only as further consequences. The French orchestra differed outstandingly from the German in one particular. As cultivated by Berlioz, Meyerbeer, and Liszt it sought to assimilate and mix all the different instrumental registers, so that there resulted a certain unity of the entire tonal body. The German orchestra also sought unity of sound as its final effect, but its three main groups always remained distinctly recognizable and the marking of the contrasts between them was important to the formal structure.

In the first half of the 19th century the German and French orchestras were the only authoritative models, the Italian orchestras remaining of less importance. Consequently Germany and France became the centres of instrumental manufacture. In earlier times, as long as the strings had headed the orchestra, Italy had been the leading country, its famous string industry being centred in North Italy, with a branch in the Tyrol. As the wind instruments developed, however, Italy lost her position of dominance. Production of the brasses was centred in Germany, of the wood-winds in France. Of course wood-winds were also produced in Germany and brasses also in France, but with time the French wood-winds and the German brasses proved superior to the same instruments as produced in other countries. Thus Italy was the native home of the strings, France of the wood-winds, Germany of the brasses.

By degrees other European countries participated in the growth of both orchestra and instruments. Spain, indeed, remained aside, and England despite her consuming activity in orchestral affairs, only in later years began making her own contribution to the production of instruments as well as works. But Russia and Austria, and more particularly Bohemia, though not yet an independent political power, showed a growing interest in orchestra and perfected their own ideas of its sonority. Russia, from the beginning of Western political influences in the 18th century long dependent upon European models, unlocked by degrees her rich sources of popular instrumental productivity and turned special attention to the brasses. Bohemia, likewise stimulated by her popular songs and dances, favored the strings and gave them new color in singing and rhythmic expression.

Thus new influxes of national provenance came to enrich the orchestra. These influences increased relatively, in accordance with the comparative differences between the given instruments in the different countries. The French brasses, for instance, being less heavily constructed than the German, continued to produce a tone more slender than that of the mighty German trumpets, trombones, even horns. The tone of the French wood-winds, on the other hand, unfolded expressive singing qualities unattainable by the German types. In accordance with these ideals of sound the instrumentalists themselves developed different qualities in the various countries. The vibrato of the French flutists, oboists, clarinetists, and bassoonists, for example, proved to be of an inimitable excellence, while in German orchestras such vibrato was long held in low repute.

Besides these differences arising out of heterogeneous national conditions, other changes were caused by new inventions and improvements in construction of the instruments. The strings, indeed, were no longer susceptible of change; the violin was a perfect type and its family complete. Some experiments to invent new types, as for instance the tenor-violin also called violetta or contra-violin, had no success. But the wood-winds and the brasses were built on mechanical principles and improvement of their mechanisms was a problem both for their makers and for the composers.

The flute, for instance, was at first quite a primitive instrument, played by covering the holes. It was improved by the addition of stops, and made larger so that its range was extended and the strength of its tone increased. In the 19th century wood was replaced by metal, usually silver, in the making of it, so that the tone of the flute, formerly often smothered by the other instruments, could better hold its own. In a similar way the key-system of the other wood-winds was developed and their construction so improved that their tones became more substantial and approached closer to the ideal.

The most important changes were those made in the brasses, especially the horns and trumpets. Originally these instruments were limited to blowing the principal tones of a single chord; they could not play a melody as soon as it contained other tones than the fundamental of the chord, its nearest relations and overtones. The key could be changed by the insertion of a crook, so that the player could move to another tonality, but of the available tones the number and relations remained the same. It was also possible to vary the pitch, especially of the horns, by stopping the bell of the horn with the hand; but in this case the quality of the tone became hollow. Also it took time either to insert the crook or to stop the bell, and the slowness of the technique of these instruments very much hampered the composer. Beethoven in *Fidelio* called for nine different tunings of the horns with 25 changes; Mozart in *Don Giovanni* for 35 changes; the number of changes Wagner asked for can hardly be counted: in the *Ring* he often ordered them from measure to measure.

These difficulties and obstructions were removed apparently at once by the invention of the valves, a system of pistons, which changed the tones by mechanical means. These valves—first two, then three—were invented in Germany as early as about 1820. The surprising excellence of the valves lay not only in the elimination of the disturbing and time-consuming gestures involved in the earlier method, but also in the fact that the range of tones was increased so that now the entire chromatic scale could be played by the horns and trumpets as by a piano.

In spite of these advantages the composers hesitated to use the valve instruments. There was much argument about this new invention. It certainly eliminated the technical difficulties, but at the same time it destroyed the bright sound of the natural horn and trumpet tones. Even Berlioz, Liszt, and Wagner still prescribed in their scores the old tunings for these instruments. Only with time did composers accept the valves, although the players themselves had already been using them during the second half of the 19th century.

The perfection of the valves was for many years the central problem of instrument makers in Germany as well as in France. One of the most influential of these men was the Belgian Sax, who flourished about 1840. The Sax-horns have become indispensable to the French orchestra because of their exact intonation and facile technique. Sax's name is best known for his invention of the saxophone, a bastard clarinet, but constructed of metal, having a conical tube with recurved bell. In spite of its curiously penetrating, mellow tone, which resembles that of the English horn, the saxophone has not become naturalized in the symphony orchestra, although it has occasionally been used, as in Richard Strauss's "Symphonia domestica." But it became most important to the development of the jazz orchestra, which was now soon to take place, and, consequently, to the latest stage of orchestral evolution.

2

IN GENERAL the development of the orchestra from about the middle of the 19th century shows extensive and intensive activity, especially in the field of mechanical invention. The fundamental type had been fixed during the first half of the century. The task of the second half was to develop and improve the separate sections, in other words, the wood-winds and brasses, these being the only two groups, apart from the percussion instruments, susceptible of further betterment to suit the intentions of composers. The composers themselves consciously or unconsciously assisted the makers. Some favored the use of military band instruments in the symphonic orchestra. Wagner called for his Nibelung-tubas, demanded a bass-trumpet, was interested in the perfection of the flute, which was also constructed as an alto-flute. In France, where, as we know, the light brasses were developed, the *cornet á pistons,* an intermediate type between trumpet and key-bugle, was, because of its technical fluency, incorporated in the French orchestra very soon after its invention. Rossini already used it in his *Guillaume Tell,* written in 1829, and both Berlioz and Meyerbeer called for it frequently.

Thus the mechanism of the orchestra was carried to completion during the second half of the 19th century but the results in the field of music varied according to national desires and sound ideals. Italy in the 17th and 18th centuries had cultivated concert compositions, resting upon the dominance of the strings. But this branch of Italian concert music dis-

THE NATIONAL ORCHESTRA

appeared almost wholly with the growing influence of the winds, and from now on all creative effort in Italy went into the opera, culminating in the two greatest Italian composers of modern times, Rossini, the representative of the first half of the 19th century, and Verdi the representative of the second half. There were other important composers between them, like Bellini, Mercadante, Donizetti, but they did nothing for the orchestra that was not indicated or carried out in Rossini's or Verdi's orchestra.

The Italian orchestra on the whole always remained a string orchestra dependent on the singing voice. It was an accompanying factor, independent only occasionally in overtures or intermezzi. So far as the use of the wind instruments is concerned, it was the French orchestra with its soft wind-voices that provided the model for the Italian orchestra. Bellini, Rossini, and Donizetti, who had all turned to Paris as the operatic centre of that time, imitated the French orchestra, changing it in detail to accord with their special needs, as, for example, Rossini did in his development of a steadily increasing crescendo. In general the dominating bel-canto style—an outstanding quality of Bellini's vocal writing—prevented the unfolding of the Italian opera orchestra, which was limited to stereotyped formulas of accompaniment that, apart from short introductions to arias, established a certain independence only by insistent rhythm.

The one exception was Rossini's *Tell* which of course left the Italian model for French grand opera. Here not only the overture with its soloistic play of the cello, the singing English horn, the virtuoso flute paraphrases, and finally the martial trumpets and the brilliant crescendo of the string Allegro, is, so to speak, a résumé of all virtuoso orchestral effects. The opera itself contains plenty of orchestral episodes which surpass all hitherto usual forms of orchestration, especially in the solo activity of single wind-instruments and the utilization of their colors.

Compared with the richly decorated orchestra Rossini used in *Tell*, Verdi's orchestra appears in his youthful operas to be a reaction toward the simpler Italian models of Bellini and Donizetti. But in proportion as Verdi withdrew from the bel-canto style —which never was his field—instead of approaching a naturalistic style of singing, he treated his orchestra differently from the way his predecessors had treated theirs. Verdi's orchestra was no longer the merely accompanying, subordinate element, although it did not strive to distinguish itself by soloistic effects. For Verdi the orchestra was primarily an organ of rhythm. Harmony remained of secondary importance, rhythm created the physiognomy and the taut, vigorous muscular system. It animated the melodic singing of the voice and gave it red-blooded vivacity, dramatic temperament, impressive force. The short introduction of *La donna è mobile*, for instance, with its apparently stereotyped chords consisting of triple rhythms, is something other than a conventional formula for accompaniment. It is at the same time the picture of the Duke's brutal recklessness and domineering temperament. It is a dramatic commentary to the scene.

Verdi changed the older operatic formulas of accompaniment into plastic media of characterization. In this direction his orchestra steadily developed with the growth of his dramatic treatment of the voice. His last period, from *Aïda* to *Othello* and *Falstaff*, points almost directly to chamber music. Even his early works prove Verdi's full knowledge and mastery of the effects of the single instrument. The conspiracy in the third act of *Ernani* (composed in 1844), with its cello solo, is a particularly colorful bit of tone-painting. Another striking instrumental piece is the duet of Rigoletto and Sparafucile at the beginning of the second act. One cello and one double-bass, both muted, play the melody, while three groups of violas, cellos and double-basses accompany and low clarinets, bassoons, and bass drum are added. It is one of the strangest orchestral pictures ever painted. Verdi frequently favors the double-bass, the most important example being the great double-bass solo when Othello enters Desdemona's chamber to murder her. There are almost innumerable examples of Verdi's clear and secure knowledge of his orchestra, from the gipsy sonorities of *Trovatore* and the witch's ballad with its whispering, ghostly rhythms to the glimmering Nile of Aïda's aria and the fire-chorus of the first act of *Othello*.

Thus for Verdi the orchestra gradually becomes a medium of dramatic expression much as it was for Wagner, save for one notable difference: Verdi's orchestra, important though it may be as a partner of the voices, always remains dependent on the action of the stage and on the singers. It never gains independence and it never becomes the root and source of the stage procedure. Occasionally it takes the melody and the voice is only inserted in parlando style, as in the duet just mentioned from *Rigoletto*; or the orchestra determines the thematic character which the voice afterwards adopts, as in Iago's credo from *Othello*; or the melody grows in the orchestra and reaches its perfection with the singer, as in the great Aïda-Amonasro duet.

But in every case the orchestra remains subservient to the stage. For the most part Verdi like Meyerbeer even avoids writing an overture; a short introduction suffices him. Nor are there any independent intermezzi in the opera, with the exception of such cases as the above-mentioned double-bass solo in *Othello*, which illustrates a scenic event. Verdi wrote no ballet music either, except in a few cases like that of *Aïda*, where the ballet was stipulated by the opera as commissioned.

On the whole Verdi's orchestra, starting from the

performance of compact harmonies, developed toward looseness of harmonic bonds. Wagner in *Parsifal* returned to the closed harmonic structure of three instrumental choirs, Verdi in *Falstaff* strove for the independence of each single orchestral voice. The instruments are frequently introduced independently one from another, not for soloistic or virtuoso purposes, but as selected representatives, so to speak, of a full chord which is hinted at only by its most characteristic instrumental color. It is a method of orchestration by abbreviation, the method of the musical dramatist who strives after the shortest, most intensified expression.

This method reaches its goal in the score of *Falstaff* which can almost be called a chamber-music score. Colors and dynamics are limited to intimations, harmony itself loses its solid objectivity, supporting the whole structure, indeed, no longer as a real scaffolding but only as an evanescent framework of underlying conceptions. Verdi's path is one of the strangest any composer ever trod. It leads from the most terrestrial starting-point toward a purely spiritual world of dramatic phantoms, and his treatment of the orchestra parallels the changes. Each color reveals its most subtle qualities, the dynamics are refined to almost improbable degrees. Verdi is not satisfied with two or three pianos, he demands four, five, six pianos. His instrumental expression overflows into a sphere of unreality, where the imagining of an effect seems to be more important than the actual sound.

Despite this high transparency there remain both the rhythmic subsoil and the function of accompaniment characteristic of Verdi's orchestra. It never becomes self-sufficient, it is always the servant of the singing voice, and the ensemble which grows up from this coöperation represents one of the greatest heights ever reached in opera. That height was reached by the passing of the Italian type of orchestra with its dominating string nature, through the illustrative and festive type of the French (Meyerbeer) orchestra, back to the national Italian model. Now it was freed from stereotyped and conventional mannerism and developed up to the last and most subtle details.

3

THE Italian orchestra, still directed by the idea of serving the voice, by thus departing toward a new chamber-music style delivered to the general tendency toward constant orchestral enlargement its first great disintegrating blow. A similar resistance was arising in France, where Berlioz' idea of orchestral abundance was also being corrected to meet the needs of the voice, which in French opera required even greater consideration because of the necessity of making the words understandable. Bizet's *Carmen*, (1875), composed a few years after Verdi's *Aïda* and the completion of Wagner's *Ring*, established the new type of French opera orchestra, an orchestra without any tendency towards expansion in either size or dynamic content, an orchestra which, like that of Verdi's later works, sought refinement of effect, lightening of the mechanical apparatus, increased flexibility and intensifying of subtle details. The principle of a single tone acting for a full harmony became dominant, one word seemed to suffice for a whole sentence, one tone of the trumpet or the flute was felt to be more important than whole periods of the full orchestra.

This was the method employed to trace quickly changing moods, incessantly varying situations, to picture naturalistic action and to follow exactly the words of the singer. Bizet's orchestra practically gave up the use of detailed forms. It employed them occasionally, as in the Toreador's song with its martial rhythms, in certain choruses, or in the Habanera and Seguedilla. But even these songs show the tendency toward loosening of the forms, to mingle them with improvisatory incidents that suddenly deviate from the supposed base-line.

The *Carmen* orchestra is always fluid, it plays about the voices, it throws some unexpected lights on them, it disappears suddenly like a subterraneous stream and breaks out again—it is no longer a solid body, it is an atmospheric thing, it creates light and darkness, brightness and shadow and changing colors, but without corporeal objectivity. The famous smuggler's quintet in the second act, the card trio in the third, show how the orchestra flows around the voices. The most important dramatic dialogue in the last act, during the decisive scene between Carmen and José, is supported in the orchestra only by some lightly applied tints, accentuations, short melodic phrases, impulses, as they must pass through the mind of the protagonist at the moment.

The wood-winds are the natural speakers of this orchestra. Their different colors make possible sudden characterization, while the strings are saved for the closed forms, or for a special kind of suggestive accompaniment as in the Habanera and Seguedilla. The wood-winds provide the dramatic elements and they are also the soloists. The introduction of the second act with the bassoon solo, anticipating José's song, that of the third act with the flute and clarinet solo, accompanied by the harp, painting the nocturne-mood of the coming scene, prove Bizet's predilection for the sonority of the wood-winds. They determine the sound-sphere of the work on the whole, most closely resembling the special timbre of French voices.

Strings as well as brasses give only the perspective and certain accents of color in this first impressionistic work, which appeared as the sharpest contradiction to the well-organized, thoughtful construction of Wagner's opera. It was also a contradiction to the opera developed from orchestra and harmony, with man as the highest representative of this organic evolution. In Bizet's *Carmen* man was the root and harmony as well as orchestra were utilized only as media to throw some light upon the background of characters and events. With *Carmen* the anti-orchestral opera had begun, in a form, indeed, which veiled the inner opposition involved and seemed an especially fortunate balance of dramatic singing and orchestral commentary.

4

AT ABOUT the same time that the formerly cosmopolitan French orchestra took on national features, other national orchestral types grew up in the Eastern part of Europe. In Bohemia Frederick Smetana (1824-1884), created a series of operas, whose language, plot, and music showed a conscious national attitude. The plots were taken from native Bohemian life, the music was based upon popular songs. The most successful and best known of these operas was *The Bartered Bride*, composed in 1866, but several of the others, such as *The Kiss, The Two Widows, Dalibor* also had success. Smetana's name became better known through a series of purely orchestral works, among which the cycle "My Fatherland" has kept alive to the present day. This cycle consists of a number of symphonic poems, each of them in one movement, a more modest musical realization of his ideals than Liszt himself had achieved.

Smetana's music springs from the primitive and

genuine source of a highly gifted and musical people, whose creative impulses, formerly limited to songs and dances, were concentrated for the first time by Smetana in a cultivated art form. Smetana's sound ideal was given by his musical heritage. He needed no unusual instruments, no particular augmentation of his orchestra. It was based upon the soft sonorities of the strings, whose melodic singing was developed from Bohemian folk-tunes and proved this origin in Smetana's predilection for doubling his melodies in thirds. The wood-winds complete this simple songlike string orchestra, the brasses being utilized for the natural dynamic climaxes, so that on the whole it is of that classic type which refers back to the models of Mozart and Haydn rather than to Beethoven.

The Bohemian landscape, the Bohemian legend were the spiritual background for Smetana's music. An inexhaustible melodic invention directed by an always genuine and naïve spiritual mastery was the source of his popular and at the same time highly artistic works. Smetana was one of those rare individuals who without any revolutionary tendencies always keep alive and even modern. This came from his immediate and natural connection with his native soil. Yet he had the artistic ability to elevate these native qualities to universal value. Smetana has frequently been called the Bohemian Mozart and this title has a certain justification, as regards not the importance of his musical genius but the perfection of his work

THE NATIONAL ORCHESTRA

on the whole and the melodious and balanced charm of his musical style.

Smetana's work was carried on by Anton Dvořák (1841-1904), who was also Bohemian. He also preserved the native ground of his musicianship, but he was a less domestic and naïve personality, and he strove for world-wide recognition. His music was influenced by Brahms, who was personally interested in Dvořák's development. So Dvořák no longer showed the simplicity of Smetana's style. He had a certain symphonic ambition, remaining nevertheless within his native limits. In contrast with the singing qualities of Smetana's melodies Dvořák favored dance-rhythms and provided greater variety in them by means of a more richly furnished orchestral style.

The last step in this Slavic group was taken by the Moravian Leo Janaček (1854-1926), whose work is represented mainly by his operas. These operas, the best known of which is *Jenufa* (1902), showed a growing trend toward developing musical style from language, so that the orchestra more and more was pressed into service as a base for musicalized language. This development did not arise, as in the case of Wagner, from the compulsions of harmony. Harmony, on the contrary, seemed to be but the accidental consequence of a musical method the aim of which was to imitate language by means of musical expression.

The Bohemian group has produced a great number

of other more or less important musicians. Whatever their diversities they all, from Suk (1874-1934), to the young Martinu, keep a certain conformity with regard to the orchestra, due mainly to their native background. Bohemian music even in its modern manifestations does not deny its relationship with domestic popular music. It is linked always with the sweet, engaging sounds of the violins, with the songful or rhythmic character of the folk-tunes. As an instrumental art it does not discover new paths but reflects familiar orchestral types in a national mirror that has particular charm.

5

SLAVIC music on the whole is primarily emotional music, moved, like the spiritual life of the people, less by intellectual forces than by imagination, inspired by melancholy or by wantness or by other feelings of the sort. The Slavic composers used no special orchestra of their own, but amended the Western European model in accordance with their differing impulses and purposes. Into Russia European music was imported very early. In the 18th century Catherine the Great maintained an Italian opera in St. Petersburg, where Cimarosa and many famous musicians were active either permanently or as guests. But this was an affair of the court, and in spite of their rich musical gifts Russian musicians only slowly came into their own.

THE NATIONAL ORCHESTRA

Michael Glinka (1804-1857) was the first to write a national opera, *A Life for the Czar*. But it was mainly the plot that was Russian, the music depended on foreign models and Glinka himself was a pupil of the Conservatory in Leipzig. The first Russian musician who consciously turned from European models to the genuine Russian sources of folk-song and church-music with its Byzantine harmonies, was Mussorgsky (1839-1881). His *Boris Godunoff*, performed in 1874, one year before *Carmen*, sprang from the impulse to give musical expression to the Russian language, so that Mussorgsky arrived at other, mainly simpler forms than the Western European composers. The emphasizing of linguistic values led him to repress both the Italian aria-style and German orchestral harmony. But in spite of his comparatively independent attitude Mussorgsky remained bound to the tradition of European opera, especially with regard to the orchestra. This dependence was enhanced by his friend Rimsky-Korsakoff, who, because Mussorgsky was an amateur, corrected and changed the orchestration of *Boris* to agree with the customary European orchestral style.

Rimsky himself belonged to a group of Russian musicians who consciously strove for independence from West-European influences. But despite their best intentions they could not wholly free themselves, because they could produce no counter-example of equal force to follow. All that happened was, as in Bohemia, that the plots of the operas, the poetic inspirations for the instrumental works were taken from the native poets, popular rhythms, characteristic harmonies, folk-tunes themselves were put to use. Native color is strong in these works but their foundation was still in Western Europe and in orchestral style in particular no basic change could be achieved.

Wagner's influence had indeed met with violent opposition and was limited, but the influence of French composers took a firmer root. Rimsky himself relied on Berlioz and Liszt; he was a friend of orchestral expansion. Most of the other Russian composers—Balakireff, Borodin, Glasunoff, Taneieff and the rest—although some of them were highly gifted, proved not strong enough to create a really independent national music. They did not succeed in replacing European influences in harmony, and consequently in the orchestra, by any new Russian style. All they could do was to establish a Russian province of European music, like the Bohemian province, apparently independent in some respect, but in reality nothing other than a national offshoot from the great tree of European musical culture.

The most outstanding figure to appear among these Russians was Peter Ilyich Tschaikovsky (1840-1893). He was the most outstanding because he was the most highly gifted, indeed—with the exception of Mussorgsky—as yet the only great Russian com-

THE NATIONAL ORCHESTRA

poser of world stature. Tschaikovsky wrote operas, symphonies with and without programs, symphonic poems and programmatic overtures. Of his numerous operas only two had a European success: *Eugen Onegin*, performed in 1878, a few years after *Boris Godunoff* and *Carmen*, and, about twelve years later, *Pique Dame*. Apart from his orchestral works with and without stage—among which some great ballets must be included—Tschaikovsky wrote no works of importance. His chamber music, his songs, and some piano works may be classed as salon-music.

Tschaikovsky's was a primitive nature, especially in matters of the mind. One might say morbid rather than primitive, for his spiritual sense reveals decay rather than growth. His programmatic works for instance were mainly built up from projects provided by his friends. The "Manfred" symphony was actually worked out from a plan by Balakireff, who even prescribed the keys. Tschaikovsky had no special interest in intellectual problems and affairs. In this respect he resembled Bruckner, although the two personalities were wholly unlike and Tschaikovsky cannot be compared to Bruckner in originality.

On the other hand, Tschaikovsky was so filled with music that everything he touched turned into music, music which came only from emotional sources and never left the sphere prescribed by them. His symphonies show the intellectual circuit of the early romantic period. They live as the reflection of the simple, personal emotions aroused by an enthusiastic, often fanatical imagination, feelings that remain misty, not clear, unintelligible even in their background and their aims. Their expression is stimulated only by a charming sense for changing colors and an instinct for overwhelming dynamics, the two qualities which made Tschaikovsky primarily an orchestral composer and which manifest themselves in his symphonies and overtures as well as in his operas with a powerful force of invention, nourished from inexhaustible musical impulses.

There was no essential difference in the media used by him and his West-European contemporaries. Tschaikovsky avoided unusual instruments. His works of course presuppose a well-furnished string group, but not the multitude demanded by Berlioz or Wagner. His harmonies are rich and spring from an abundant sense of sonority, though the chromatics are only interwoven with and subordinate to the diatonic melodic line, the juicy fullness which characterizes the harmonies coming rather from the fullness of the orchestral setting, the well-chosen mixture of the brasses and the wood-winds with the strings generally in the lead.

Tschaikovsky's effects further arise from his primary impetus toward rhythmic and dynamic development on a large scale, as shown in one of his most impressive compositions, the marchlike third movement of his last symphony (No. 6), called the

TSCHAIKOVSKY

THE NATIONAL ORCHESTRA

"Pathétique," probably because of the strange character of the Finale, which slowly grows and disappears in a dusk of melancholy and resignation. There are other special effects like the ingeniously sketched pizzicato Scherzo from the Fourth symphony; there are sometimes motives stalking through the whole work like an *idée fixe*, as in the Fifth symphony. In these and similar cases Tschaikovsky favors the trombones and trumpets; they are to him the voices of the fates. His energy as a composer lives on the idea that the impressiveness of a musical effect depends upon the loudness of its execution.

Tschaikovsky's orchestra, like Smetana's, was on the whole a homophonic orchestra. One could set down a complete score on a single staff. This orchestra has a charm and a naïveté very similar to Smetana's. It also shows the same intrusion of national elements into symphonic writing. In Tschaikovsky's orchestra these national elements manifested themselves in the emphasizing of certain native sound effects, in the use of the strings as foundation, the wood-winds as colorful decoration, the brasses as dynamic accents. This was the type of the early romantic orchestra, belonging to the period before Wagner and Brahms, a counterpart to Weber's German national orchestra, growing up now among the newly awakened Slavic peoples, proclaiming their desire to participate in the creation of music.

6

Not only the Slavic peoples participated with increasing interest in the development of orchestral culture. Composers in other countries, hitherto inactive or satisfied with modest tasks, applied themselves to the writing of symphonies. Among the Englishmen some notable personalities stepped forth to the production of great orchestral works: the late Sir Edward Elgar (born in 1857), and Frederick Delius (1863-1934), Granville Bantock (1868-) and Vaughan Williams (1872-) became the chief representatives of a new school of English composers. Jenó Hubay (1858-), Ernest Dohnanyi (1877-), Bela Bartók (1881-), and Zoltan Kodály (1882-) have created a special Hungarian school. The Scandinavian countries produced Niels W. Gade (1817-1890), Edward Grieg (1843-1907), Christian Sinding (1856-), Carl Nielsen (1865-), Kurt Atterberg (1887-). To-day, the most important and widely known of these nationally rooted composers is the Finn Jean Sibelius (1865-), who has already written seven symphonies and a large group of other instrumental works. Sibelius is at present perhaps the most generally recognized and most performed living symphonist—especially in the Anglo-Saxon countries, the Middle-European countries not caring as much for his music—his work as a whole representing an imposing contribution to the symphonic production of the present time.

THE NATIONAL ORCHESTRA

Strange as it may seem, in the same measure as the musical moods and thematic material used by all these nationally rooted composers shows its relationship to native poetry, legends, landscapes, their orchestras lose their special domestic features and approach a certain similarity of technique and expression. Nationality seems to have determined the attitude of these composers and opened to them new spiritual resources. But for their orchestral medium they accepted the West-European models. They added some new tint from their own national palette, giving the old familiar orchestra certain new colors. But the conventional symbols remained as they had been fixed by their predecessors, so that these national works of art, like those simultaneously composed in Europe, show a retrospective tendency.

The growing number and variety of new creative temperaments revealed in these national manifestations of purely emotional origin added momentum to the general trend in European orchestral music. The rational framework of the orchestra and its forms had been exhausted and the process of dissolution into purely emotional display was proceeding irresistibly.

X

The "Art-for-Art's-Sake" Orchestra of *Strauss, Debussy, Puccini*

I

A LIST of the composers who have written for orchestra shows three different types; first, those who wrote mainly operas; second, those who wrote mainly for instrumental concerts; third, those whose creative activity embraced both stage and concert hall. Lully, Gluck, Grétry, Spontini, Weber, Meyerbeer, Rossini, Bellini, Wagner, Verdi, Bizet, Puccini wrote operas only—to mention but the most important names. This is the line of the musical dramatists. Bach, Stamitz, Haydn, Beethoven, Mendelssohn, Schumann, Liszt, Brahms, Bruckner, Mahler, Reger, Sibelius, Elgar wrote chiefly concert music. This is the line of the symphonists. Monteverdi, Purcell, Rameau, Handel, Mozart, Cherubini, Berlioz, Gounod, Smetana, Mussorgsky, Tschaikovsky, Debussy, Strauss, Schoenberg, Stravinsky wrote both opera and concert music in about equal quantities.

Comparing these three groups, we see that there have always been, since its beginning, composers

"ART-FOR-ART'S-SAKE" ORCHESTRA

chiefly interested in opera, and that there have always been composers interested in both concert and opera, but that the middle group of composers, who created mainly concert music, that is to say, the group of the symphonists, embraces only a limited period of about 150 years. This period reached its height very quickly with Beethoven, whose only opera, *Fidelio,* represents rather an operatic symphony. From Beethoven we see the spread of symphonic art not as a culmination but in many subdivisions, defined in the end along national lines. In all other fields of musical activity the development shows an up-and-down and again upward swing. Mozart was indeed a genius of singular importance in opera, but both Wagner and Verdi created works of a new type and achieved world-wide success. Thus the species opera has always been renewed within itself; other models were created which could be compared to the classic model.

In symphonic art a certain extension took place, combined with variations of detail. But not even the most important and successful new productions could ever be compared to the unique apparition of Beethoven, and the highest condition later composers have been able to reach is designation as a successor of Beethoven. No matter to whom this title has been given, the fact alone of its bestowal proves that Beethoven even today is regarded as having set the unsurpassed standard of symphonic music. This acknowledgment is not only a moral one, it is confirmed by our actual concert programs, the nucleus and chief contents of which are Beethoven's works.

That this should be the case in a creative period embracing some 150 years is not to be explained only by the overwhelming genius of Beethoven or the lack of gifts in later generations. It is a condition laid down by the general character of the orchestral symphony itself, that is to say, by other than its musical qualities. The symphony was not a purely musical affair. Its creation hung upon certain intellectual and social conditions, and the invariability of the symphonic type up to the present day proves that the symphony was and is bound by them for all time. These conditions themselves may have functioned from changing points of view. The composers of the 19th century did make, so to speak, a circle around Beethoven as its centre until they finished in national aspects. But the centre itself always remained the same, founded upon a common consciousness, intellectual, spiritual, even religious, which might express itself in a variety of social offshoots. New stimuli could be gained only by delving into those resources which led to the exposition of poetic and at last of national feeling. But the potentialities in these directions were limited and could in no case bring about any essential change in the social and intellectual and consequently the artistic foundation of the symphony.

It was and remained a retrospective sort of musical

"ART-FOR-ART'S-SAKE" ORCHESTRA

activity with the more or less consciously kept centre of Beethoven. Consequently the orchestral ideal of Beethoven could be varied by manifold means, but it never could be replaced by any other orchestral ideal, as Mozart's operatic ideal has been replaced by several other operatic ideals during the 19th century. The symphonic orchestra was established for good and all by Beethoven, and in so far Wagner was right when he declared symphonic production after Beethoven to be superfluous. He forgot, perhaps, or overlooked, the numerous possibilities of variation, but the theme itself he knew could not be changed.

There was only one field of musical activity from which new stimulus for the orchestra could be acquired: opera. Opera was an older, a richer, a more multifarious and therefore more changeable organism than the symphony. Opera had run through the most various stages and had accommodated itself to the most different social conditions. It had been the representative of aristocratic as well as of popular societies, it could accept international and national features, it was as changeable as clothing; it had no character of its own, wherefore it could reflect any other character. Opera changed its point of view in accordance with the changes in other fields of life. In opera therefore at the end of the 19th century the orchestra was obliged to find new stimuli.

The social background of opera at all times had been that of entertainment, directed by the particular need of each epoch. The desire might be to reconstruct Greek drama, as it was from the first Florentine operas up to Monteverdi, Lully, Rameau, Gluck, and Spontini. Or to exploit the art of prominent singers, as in the Italian operas of the 17th and 18th centuries. Or to criticize social life, as it was in Mozart's works, or to declare the ethics of heroism, as in Beethoven's *Fidelio*, or mystical romanticism, as in Wagner's creations. Between and among these there were many other types of opera, each the centre of a common interest and indicative of a common need for musical entertainment.

About the end of the 19th century these needs lost by degrees all their peculiarly social features. Art in general and music in particular became commodities which could be bought by anybody, who had money enough to pay for them. The value of the art-work no longer depended on its importance to the community, on the ability of the artist to reveal the unconscious impulses of the common life and to express them in artistic forms. The artist and the musician were no longer universal voices. They were only individuals trying, by the artistic value, so-called, of their work, to win the attention of certain circles interested in creative production; and this value was arrived at by comparison with traditional values and was influenced by the artist's peculiar gifts for innovation. This was the period of "art-for-art's-sake."

The phrase "art-for-art's-sake" implies that an

artistic work has no other purpose than the enjoyment of its production and its existence. The idea of creation for any other purpose, such as Bach's when he wrote his Passions and Cantatas for his parish in Leipzig, or Beethoven's when he wrote his works inspired by the ideas of freedom and human community, or even Wagner's, when he wrote for an invisible circle of people who "felt a common need" —such former ideas were looked upon as extraneous to the essential being of the work of art. This work of art existed by itself and for itself alone, it must be perfect according to the rules of experience and the possibilities of imagination. Its task was alone to please men by the fact of its existence and in this way to divert their spirits from all remembrance of reality and elevate them into a sphere of absolute art.

The principle of art-for-art's-sake has often been discussed, and always both hailed and scorned. It originated in France, and the idea of *l'art-pour-l'art* stands for an appreciation of art which acknowledges every kind of art as a decoration or ornament of life. This is certainly just as sound an idea as the contrary idea, which recognizes art as the transfiguration of life, a sublimation of the events or the impulses of life. They are two different manifestations of the creative will, nothing else. Consequently neither can be designated as better or less good than the other.

But history shows that these two ideas generally alternate. Periods in which powerful impulses prevail produce an art directed toward similar aims, while periods that have no spiritual centre incline to emphasize the so-called purely artistic values. The appearance of the latter sort of period for the most part signifies the beginning of a decay; but on the other hand, the frequently overrated periods of ethically founded art often lack the capacity to distinguish between genuine and false art, because they take their standard not from the art itself but from the convictions of the artists. Thus they frequently alter both the intention and the achievement.

The classic period of music in the 18th century had united both qualities and therefore it was called classic, that is, balanced. But then the mighty impulse that came from Beethoven had driven his successors forward in the direction of exploiting ethical ideas. Now the stimuli coming from this impetus had been exhausted, a reaction followed. The medium itself became purpose, art isolated itself, and the completion of all technical and mechanical tools became the new goal.

The orchestra seemed to be the most suitable apparatus for the unfolding of such purely artistic tendencies. The orchestra had always been a mechanically constructed organism, so that imputing to it a creative principle that was in the main mechanically directed seemed but natural, other principles having been exhausted in the process of development. The fundamental laws had been discovered. Ethics had had their day, the endeavors they had inspired had become entangled in conventional symbols, the increased consciousness of social community was not contributing fruitful influences, was indeed itself progressively decaying. Now those who were masters of the apparatus itself appeared and called forth once again the whole spell of the orchestra, with the sole aim of enhancing the charm of this modern branch of musical art. For this awakening, this new ideal of orchestra, the opera was responsible.

2

THERE are three composers whose creative work sums up these tendencies: Richard Strauss, Claude Debussy, Giacomo Puccini, one a German, one a Frenchman, one an Italian, each of them the last of a finishing or dying generation, each of them a true representative of his time and his countrymen. There is still a fourth, too, a Russian, to complete the number of the leading musical nations: Stravinsky. But he belongs not wholly in this group and already has turned from its summarizing retrospection to new aims.

But the work of these three, born nearly at the same time—Puccini in 1858, Debussy in 1862, Strauss in 1864—represents the last résumé of that great orchestral music which had been the axis of all musical production since Beethoven's time. In a way they might be compared to the earlier group of orchestral virtuosi—Berlioz, Meyerbeer, Liszt; indeed, important features are common to both groups. But while the earlier group consists of enterprising, conquering personalities advancing into unknown regions, the later group looks back to the past. They appeared to be innovators and when their works were first performed timid souls thought them revolutionary. But with time this sort of revolution appears to have been only an illusion, caused by some novel arrangement of the elements of traditional art.

This tradition itself remained unaltered, and at present we realize that any new movements must arise from conditions other than those that produced Strauss, Debussy, and Puccini, in whom we acknowledge once again the psychological, the atmospheric, the sensuous musician—in short, the type of musical genius that takes its formative principles from emotional impulses. This was the line leading from Beethoven up—or down—the various spurs of the romantic century. The other line, starting from the rational impulses of the 18th century, had not yet been continued. The orchestra that could take up this line must be organized on other principles than those of color and dynamics.

Thus Strauss, Debussy, and Puccini are end-points and their works look back. They are nationally conditioned works, masterly in form, carried out with such magnificent superiority that together they represent the essence of European musical culture, and more particularly of the orchestral art, of their century.

In his new edition of Berlioz' treatise on orchestration Strauss remarks: "I advise all my young colleagues to go into the tuning room of the orchestra and to study what the musicians are playing there, when they feel unobserved. In this way one can learn what the instruments can do in reality." These words are valuable, because of the truth they contain and the reference to practice by one of the best practitioners of music, himself the son of an orchestra musician. But they are also characteristic and informative in that they reveal the origin of many of Strauss's own inspirations. Beethoven never would have spoken in this way. "Do you mean that I think of your miserable violin if the spirit speaks to me?" he answered when Schuppanzigh complained of a difficult violin-passage. For Beethoven the idea came first, the question of execution remained secondary. Works by Strauss frequently suggest that the idea of the single effect preceded the idea of the work as a whole, and even that certain works have grown from the perception of certain instrumental effects.

This observation is not to be taken as deprecatory. The fact would naturally result from the principle of art-for-art's-sake, which starts with some artistic invention and seeks occasions for its use. Strauss's knowledge of the instruments was astonishing and surpassed even that of the players themselves. His treatment of the horn—his father's instrument—and other winds of all kinds revealed qualities hitherto unknown. It is characteristic of Strauss that his main interest was directed not toward the invention of new instruments but toward the re-introduction of old types. In *Elektra* he used the basset-horn, forgotten since the time of Mozart, and prescribed the Wagner tubas for the solemn scene of Oreste's appearance; in the "Symphonia domestica" he used the old oboe d'amore—an intermediate type between the modern oboe and the English horn—for the characterization of the "child," and furthermore a quartet of saxophones; in *Till Eulenspiegel* he used the rattle and in *Woman Without a Shadow* the Bohemian glass-harmonica. Besides these reminders of old instruments he used some new types, as in *Salome* and the "Alpine" Symphony, the Heckelphone, a kind of baritone-oboe, invented in 1904 by the instrument-maker Heckel. Furthermore there was the celesta, invented in 1886, in Paris, by Mustel—a kind of carillon, consisting of metal bars, played by keys, and producing a mysterious, soft, glittering sound which Strauss used to great advantage in *Rosenkavalier* at the presentation of the silver rose. The celesta has been very frequently used in the modern orchestra because of its incorporeal and melting sounds. The prelude from Schreker's *Die Gezeichneten* shows how exciting the effect of the celesta combined with muted strings may be.

Strauss knew not only the technique of the usual,

the special charm of the unusual instruments and the art of mingling their tones. He knew also that the secret of such effects did not lie in the number of instruments and the size of the orchestra, but that the small orchestra too could produce new and surprising effects if the instruments were handled and combined in the proper way. From his first orchestral works up to *Salome, Elektra* and *Rosenkavalier* his orchestration showed an increasing number of voices and colors. Then, in accordance with a new tendency towards simplification and an older melodic style, a sudden reaction set in. The *Ariadne* orchestra showed a chamber-music combination, the number of musicians being restricted to 36, and mass-effects were replaced by soloistic uses of the separate voices. Strauss did not keep to this line, however. *Woman Without a Shadow* resumed the earlier manner but with emphasis on virtuoso concert effects, *Intermezzo* returned to the *Ariadne* style, while the later works such as *The Egyptian Helen* and *Arabella* show mixtures of all his preceding orchestral types.

Evidently Strauss himself has no precise ideal for orchestral sonority; he plays with most contrary types, and proves his absolute mastery in doing whatever he wants. His desires do not arise from inner necessities, they are fortuitous, so that he seeks the most various causes to satisfy his impulse for experiment and invention. His technical method is based upon Wagner's Leitmotiv technique, on the division and reunion of the elements of harmony, presented by themes, which however are melodically more complete than Wagner's. Harmony loses its fundamental and cosmic importance and becomes again the medium for joining the single voices in accordance with a system of pseudo-polyphony. But the character of this music is purely homophonic. There are single melodic base-lines and harmony only provides the shadings that deepen the perspective.

3

THE principle behind this leveling of the musical elements was psychological, even psycho-analytical. It ruled Strauss's conceptions from the start and led him from his first orchestral compositions to the field of opera. One might say that Strauss's tone-poems from "Don Juan," "Till Eulenspiegel" and "Death and Transfiguration" to "Heldenleben" are in reality operas without words, while his later operas, from *Salome* to *Rosenkavalier, Ariadne, Woman Without a Shadow* and the subsequent works, are orchestral compositions which involve the singing voices. In every case words or thoughts were stimuli for the technical development and sonority of the orchestra, and in every case the voices themselves have become assistants to orchestral expression.

Thus the inner content of the action gave the impulse for psychological or psycho-analytical treatment of the orchestra, and this orchestra remained

"ART-FOR-ART'S-SAKE" ORCHESTRA

the true and perfect representative of all that happened. From this enhancement of orchestra by the action there resulted the most astonishing effects: the high piercing B-flat of the double-basses when Salome listens into the well for the sound of John the Baptist's head being cut off, or the paintings of Herod's neurotic visions, or (one of the most ingenious things Strauss ever wrote) the mysterious chord—c-sharp, a-sharp, e, f-double-sharp, g-sharp—of the deep winds beyond the high a-b-flat trill, when Salome has kissed the severed head.

These were the results of the art-for-art's-sake principle applied to orchestra. Orchestra was no longer an independent medium, ruled by dynamics or color for the free play of imagination. It had become a slave to stimulatory ideas from psycho-analytical fields, an apparatus of extraordinary perfection to execute the most difficult tasks. All kinds of color, of dynamics, of mechanical inventions were united here and handled with unchallenged superiority; but orchestra had lost its own importance and its own goal and had become a medium for the reproduction of any and all purposes totally unrelated to its own being.

It was indeed a wonderful apparatus, but it no longer had anything to do with its own original qualities. It had lost its magic, its cosmic importance, had become a merely mechanical phenomenon. Freed from its creative impulses this apparatus continued its run alone, driven only by the law of perseverance. As it ran it fell over and produced the most astonishing effects, but it lost its interior support and more and more became only an entertaining succession of curious and surprising feats. This organic contradiction resulted from the fact that obviously the subject of this art was an emotional process, while the form it took was of merely casual origin.

In Strauss's later works, beginning with *Rosenkavalier*, the singing voice has affected his style of orchestration in increasing measure. The phrases have acquired a smoother and better-proportioned line, so that the interweaving of the instruments with the voices has lost its jerky character and gained more symmetry. A turning toward the archaic—from the beginning one of the characteristic traits of this apparent revolutionary—has become evident and the orchestra, formerly overstuffed with secondary voices and a patchwork of related motives has gained clarity and transparency.

In reality this process has reflected not only the greater maturity of Strauss's creative abilities but mainly his growing practical experience with the orchestra. He more frequently doubles the instruments in octaves, 6th, or 3rds, omitting or simplifying the added voices. But by these means the musical substance itself is more and more thinned out and the flatness of the harmonic background becomes more clearly apparent. *Rosenkavalier* and *Ariadne*, the works which immediately follow the great climaxes of *Salome* and *Elektra,* show the best balance. *Salome* and *Elektra* themselves are the highly remarkable manifestations of an almost unlimited imagination in orchestral sonority, filled out and carried along by the gift for converting all things into orchestral tone: the shrieks of quarrelling Jews as well as the ray of moonlight caught up in the opening passage of a clarinet, the voluptuous excitation of Salome's dancing as well as the solemn emotion in the recognition of Elektra and Orestes. But various as the occasions may be and much as the musical style consequently changes from the tumultuous outbursts of the *Elektra* orchestra to the classic simplicity of the women's trio in *Rosenkavalier* or the final duet from *Ariadne,* it is orchestra as a mechanism that always remains the heart of Strauss's music and action. Text, psychology are all only stimuli to call forth the spell of this orchestra.

4

IF STRAUSS was the instrumental artist to whom harmony was an obvious but subordinate necessity of his orchestral language, Debussy was the harmonic artist and the instruments received their value to him from their ability to reflect and alter harmonic colors. Strauss's orchestra was based upon the brasses, although Strauss learned with time how to soften their crushing heaviness. Debussy, the Frenchman, started from the wood-winds and their amalgamation with the strings. The horns and trumpets were involved in his prevalent wood-wind character. Even dynamic culminations in which all brass groups participated never changed the fundamental quality of the Debussy orchestra, which seemed to be a modernized organ constructed from the wood-wind registers.

This organ type may have been derived from César Franck, the Belgian organist and composer (1822-1890). Franck's works, although dependent on Berlioz as well as on Wagnerian after-effects, represent a conscious turning away from orchestral enlargement and complication, replacing the tendency to expansion with a new contraction of the instrumental lines and simplification of the mechanism in favor of harmonic intensification. Opinion is divided on Franck's creative importance. His individual achievement was obviously to a certain extent bound to the French type of musical appreciation, as Bruckner's was restricted to a specially German perception of music. Nevertheless Franck's stimulating, purifying, and educating influence, especially on the young generation of French composers growing up under the mighty shadow of Wagner's art, can hardly be overrated.

This influence was continued by Franck's pupil Vincent d'Indy, a more didactic than originally creative personality. In spite of evident stimuli received

"ART-FOR-ART'S-SAKE" ORCHESTRA

by Wagner he was, like Franck, a mentor for young French composers to save them from imitating foreign models and to help them rediscover and keep their own path. In its ideal of sound this path led away from the cosmic orchestra with its strongly accentuated, massive brass colors and its metaphysical interpretation of the orchestral organism. Instead of this German orchestral ideology a return to former French ideals was proclaimed. This meant a return to the tonal language which Rameau had already cultivated, based, as we have seen, upon the declamatory rules of spoken language, always the foundation of French culture in every field of musical activity.

This French language sought a harmonic clothing which should reflect each emotional impulse and wrap the declamatory melodic line in changing, gliding sonorities. The ideal performer of such atmospheric harmonies, short of the organ itself, was an orchestra formed in accordance with the fundamental principles of the French organ. This organ strove not for dynamic power or contrast, but for manifold gradations within a limited range. It revolved about the same atmospheric tone ideal which determined the character of harmony itself and its relation to the French language.

Thus this French orchestra was identical with harmony itself, but in a manner which differed from the Wagnerian orchestra as the French appreciation of the phenomenon of harmony differed from the German. For the German composer harmony was the source and deepest root from which his musical world sprang up; for the French composer it was the atmospheric radiation surrounding like a soft and glittering veil the linguistic kernel of his music.

5

Debussy's acknowledgment of this difference was accelerated by two factors: his instinctive defense against the growing influence of Wagner, and his acquaintance with Mussorgsky's music, especially *Boris* which was based upon ideas of the relationship of musical language to orchestral harmony very similar to those that were developing in Debussy. The word seemed to be the creative centre. Harmony appeared to be an x-ray of language, or the prismatic refraction of the creative word. Orchestra had to be organized in such a way as to reflect this ethereal phenomenon of harmony. The more subtle the language, the words, the thoughts and intellectual conceptions, the more refined should be both harmony and orchestra.

Debussy therefore was obliged to seek always greater refinement of moods and of inspiration from the word, as Strauss was obliged to seek always more complex psychological conceptions. For both, orchestra became the ultimate expression, performance in orchestral terms the ultimate purpose.

In this way Debussy arrived at so poetic a subject

as Maeterlinck's "Pelléas et Mélisande," a drama of suspended, unpronounced emotions, which only through the music gained a certain solidity. Or he wrote orchestral works with obvious programs of a mystic sort, such as the three symphonic sketches "La Mer" ("From dawn till noon on the sea—Sport of the waves—Dialogue of the wind and the sea"), or the three "Images" ("Gigues-Iberia-Rondes de printemps"), or the three "Nocturnes," ("Nuages, fétes, sirénes"), or "L'Après-midi d'un faune"—this last perhaps the most essential of his orchestral works. Debussy never wrote a symphony, too solid form being repugnant to the particular quality of his art. An intellectual relative of Robert Schumann, he favored the sketch, not for any insufficiency of modelling— his latin sense for form protected him from this danger—but for its implication of evanescent ideas.

Debussy's own words confirm this. His explanatory notes for "Nocturnes" say that "the term should be viewed as signifying all that is associated with diversified impressions and special lights," in "Nuages" he thought of "the unchanging aspect of the sky, with the slow and melancholy passage of the clouds dissolving in a gray vagueness tinged with white," and in "Fétes" he imagined "the restless dancing rhythms of the atmosphere, interspersed with abrupt scintillations. There is also an incidental procession —a wholly visionary pageant—passing through and blended with the argent revelry, but the background of uninterrupted festival persists: luminous dust participating in the universal rhythm."

These words not only apply to the works concerned, but convey a good idea of Debussy's point of view in general. It is that of the old French program music, as already cultivated by Rameau's contemporary Couperin, but without Couperin's compact realism which portrayed single personalities and their more or less attractive individual qualities. Debussy avoided such definite descriptions, letting them dissolve in spiritual reflections, the subjects themselves reappearing in a play of soft nebulous imagination.

The orchestra had to be formed and treated accordingly. Debussy favored all veiled colors. The strings are often muted, flageolet-effects are frequently used, among the wood-winds the flute and English horn dominate with soloistic figures, other members of the orchestra being subordinate. There is no exact thematic development, but separate colorful phrases are sprinkled throughout. There are pedal-like harmonies, tremoli of the strings, among which the melancholy tones of the cellos stand out while the violins hang back. The brasses must always be heard as French brasses, not so powerful as the German, but with the tender, emasculated tones of the French brass group. One of Debussy's most important instruments is the celesta, whose "celestial" atmospheric tones dominate his orchestra and make it more than ever like an ideal French organ.

"ART-FOR-ART'S-SAKE" ORCHESTRA

Debussy's dynamics accord with this organization of the orchestra. The base-line of his works moves not towards a crescendo but towards a decrescendo. His climax, in other words, shows an anti-Beethovenian line, is an extinction, a dissolution, a fading away. This is to Debussy the highest culmination of musical expression.

This fading away indeed is characteristic of Debussy's whole artistry. The phenomenon of orchestra which had sprung from the bringing together and the interaction of all its elements had reached a stage where its purpose was the contrary of what it had originally been. It had become, so to speak, a contradiction in itself, and its organism was treated from points of view which drove it in just the reverse of its original direction. This was the result of its utilization as a medium of art-for-art's-sake, this mightiest and most far reaching instrument being changed into an organ of most intimate and absolute character. Artistically this was a highly astonishing and most admirable result, but so far as concerns the creative idea behind the orchestra it showed that composers had lost the consciousness of their instrument's true destination. The orchestra had become a mere apparatus for the demonstration of artistic mastery, the motives of which no longer had any organic relation with the fundamental qualities of the medium itself.

6

STRAUSS's development led from instrumental works to opera in which he found his most stimulating medium. Debussy wrote but a single opera, when he was about 40, but this work, *Pelléas et Mélisande*, represented the essence and entire scope of his musical being and his later orchestral works were merely partial expositions of the contents of this one opera. The third of this group, Puccini, wrote only operas. As a musician he may appear less ingenious than Debussy or Strauss. Nevertheless his importance as typifying the final appearance of Italian opera makes him as significant as both of his contemporaries. Strauss was the instrumentalist, Debussy was the harmonist, Puccini was the melodist and in his orchestra the multiplicity of orchestral voices is reduced to an absolutely homophonic style.

Puccini, the Italian, heard all music only as the singing of a single voice. Hence his orchestra was permitted only to support this voice and enhance its effects. Earlier Italian composers had, as we have seen, been directed by the same aim; Bellini, Donizetti also had written only for the singing voice, their orchestras giving the harmonic foundation. Verdi had filled this foundation with rhythmic impulses, achieving in this way the dramatic character of his opera, which he had refined with the assistance of the orchestra to chamber-music transparency of action and characters.

Puccini needed neither harmonic support nor transparency of dramatic events. His aim was only to convey emotion and make it credible, and the medium for this expression was melody, melody which contained in itself its harmonic interpretation and which must be made as telling as possible by means of the orchestra. Consequently his music was built upon the homophonic principle, like the music of Strauss and Debussy. All three composers started from different points, all three sought—consciously or not—the same goal. If Puccini wrote his famous fifths at the beginning of the second act of *Bohème*, they were no longer fifths in the sense of harmonic voice-leading, but represented only a single tone with underlying orchestral color which appeared in the form of a divided chord.

Some one tone always dominates in Puccini's orchestration. If Butterfly sings her *"Per non morire al primo,"* the wood-winds or all the strings in unison support the melody, only two trumpets making certain harmonies. Puccini's orchestral scores at first glance look like piano scores. Nearly all the instruments play the melody together with the voice, only a few side-voices—frequently the harp or two horns or violas—providing the harmony in a modest manner. It is the same in all Puccini's scores, *Butterfly* as well as *Tosca, Bohème*—with the exception of *Manon* the earliest of his yet performed operas—occasionally shows, especially in the second act at the café Momus, a more animated musical set-up; but it seems that Puccini himself found this style too complicated and consciously turned to a simpler kind of writing.

Consequently this apparently primitive orchestral style must be regarded as evidence of a special refinement. If Puccini avoided the development of motives and even a dominantly harmonic construction, he did so not for lack of capacity but because neither method was suited to him, either would have disturbed him. Therefore he used them only in a few characteristic episodes, such as the chords with treble and bass going in opposite directions at mention of the secret well in *Tosca*, or similar passages in the second act of *Bohème*, or the amusing episode in *Gianni Schicchi* when the four muted horns blow descending and ascending sevenths chords *"con voce nasale."* At the beginning of this last-named opera he even makes the kettledrums the media of harmony, when they play the fifth b-flat-f, while above them only the bassoon has the melody and the two flutes—beyond the bassoon—accompany. Another characteristic episode is the famous letter-melody from *Butterfly*, especially when it is repeated at the end of the second act by the soloistic viola d'amore and chorus *"a bocca chiusa"* behind the scenes, the up-beat being made by the celli pizzicato, while the harmony is given by clarinets and harp (*"lasciar vibrato"*).

"ART-FOR-ART'S-SAKE" ORCHESTRA

Such examples prove that Puccini knew very well the charm of characteristic harmony and the secrets of special instrumental effects. But for him they were only of secondary importance. The main thing was to make the singer's voice as sensuous as possible, to enhance its natural qualities by means of the instruments. Puccini was seldom satisfied with the effect of the voice alone; he incessantly varied its colors and therewith its expressive powers. The instruments became, as it were, a part of the voices themselves. His combinations of voices and instruments are often amazing and uncustomary, as when in Tosca's prayer the bassoon parallels the soprano. But in general most of the instruments available are united in the presentation of the melody, which in this way achieves its multicolored and most sensuous expression.

On the whole, then, Puccini made the orchestra a singing instrument, not, as Mozart did, by developing the individualities of the instruments, but on the contrary by almost unconditional adaptation and amalgamation of the orchestra's voice with the human voice. Thus the human voice represents the melody in so far as it speaks the words, while the instruments simultaneously interpret the emotional content. This method demands unusually graduated dynamics, so that Puccini frequently writes p, pp, and ppp at the same time for different instrumental groups, much as Strauss does—Strauss in order to accent the diverse motives in accord with their importance, Puccini in order to balance the melodic and the purely harmonic voices. His dynamics, like those of Debussy, frequently culminate in a sudden surprising downward trend toward a pp; usually the wood-winds develop the climax, the strings accompany with syncopations or figurations, and then suddenly the winds grow dumb and the soft sound of the strings remains alone.

Puccini's work was the third great example of a treatment of orchestra which in its final consequences turned against the original nature of orchestra. Plenty of new effects were discovered in this way, while the mastery of each of these three musicians, Strauss, Debussy, Puccini, clarified once again the full importance of the different national types. But there can be no doubt, that these composers themselves were the closing figures of a period. No German symphonist of overwhelming importance has come after Strauss, no French harmonist after Debussy, no Italian melodist and opera composer after Puccini.

This means not that music had finished with them, but that the harmonic system which they represented had lost its creative force. The orchestra as it had developed in accordance with this harmonic system had reached a point beyond which further continuation in the same direction seemed no longer possible. Through Strauss, Debussy, and Puccini this orchestra had become a toy, filled and carried no longer by the impetus of its own nature but by application to other purposes. It had become a medium for psychological,

"ART-FOR-ART'S-SAKE" ORCHESTRA

atmospheric, sensuous impulses, derived for the most part from opera. The orchestra had become the servant of these tendencies, a very clever servant, it is true, attracting attention to itself and frequently casting forgetfulness over the object of its services.

But in reality orchestra was running into oblivion. It lacked a goal. It had developed its highest abilities, had revealed its most secret spell. And now, at this zenith of mechanical achievement, there was no longer any genuine task to employ all these dexterities. They served only art-for-art's-sake.

XI

The Mechanistic Orchestra of *Schoenberg, Stravinsky* and The Present Time

I

While the creative impulse of the orchestra as developed during the 19th century was losing its driving impetus, the institution of the orchestra as a social, economic, and educational organization gained ground. The trend towards the popularization of music paralleled similar tendencies in other fields, especially in the fine arts. It was a natural consequence of the democratic and educational tendencies which spread through all countries during the second half of that century, and furthermore of the fact that the huge stock of art-works of all kinds required some systematic elaboration. The appreciation of works of art became a matter of knowledge. The quantity of works at hand was too great to justify individual opinion of their value, and different, even contradictory, as they were, historic and scientific consideration became necessary to an appreciation of their varieties and relationships, individual judgment being reserved for new creations.

THE MECHANISTIC ORCHESTRA

But the number of new creations was now small in comparison with the countless works of preceding periods, and it was these latter that attracted the most attention. Separated from the social conditions of their origin, they were taken as creations founded only on themselves; art-for-art's-sake continued to be the standard of appreciation and it applied to all existing works. Consequently there was no place for the appreciation of works as expressions of the immediate spiritual attitude of their own day and community. Everything was good as soon as it corresponded with the general laws of art. The historical ideal dominated. Sound enough in principle, this ideal was quite unproductive in the field of further creative development.

The great collection of musical compositions was exhibited as in a museum, the audiences walking from one hall or one period to another. These audiences appreciated everything, but because of this very catholicity of understanding they lost their active power of participation. They were connoisseurs, not collaborators. Their heritage was so capriciously varied that its mere administration absorbed all their creative forces. Current production claimed little interest in comparison and fell to a secondary consideration.

This shifting of interests to a mainly retrospective attitude endowed the task of reproducing musical works with a new importance. The work itself being an established fact, performance became the chief point of attention. Consequently all the media were examined and compared, and all productive forces were directed towards perfection of the performance. This was true of both soloists and ensembles and primarily true with regard to the orchestras. The standard of efficiency of the players was raised, virtuosi who would formerly have tried to proclaim themselves soloists now became members of orchestras, the musical high-schools arranged educational classes for orchestral musicians—the brass players in particular, whose education had formerly been left fortuitously in the hands of town-band or military musicians, by degrees receiving a systematic education—and the standard of the orchestra on the whole was developed in every respect.

One of the most important conditions for the achievement of these higher orchestral standards was the economic security of the orchestra. The conviction grew up that institutions of such importance to the community must be supported by the community. In the European countries, cities in particular and states as well took upon themselves the burden for the economic security of their orchestras, more recently defraying them from their radio revenues; in America the guarantees came from private individuals, yet they were sufficient to create the groundwork for the economic existence of a handsome number of large orchestras. More and more the opinion grew that responsibility for the orchestra must be a public affair, that the importance of an orchestra equalled that of schools and museums. Orchestra is no longer the pet of aristocratic amateurs, as in the 18th century, nor the object of commercial speculation on the part of enterprising men, nor have the musicians had to care for themselves as in the 19th century. Orchestra is acknowledged a fit object of public concern because it serves public interests.

Supported by public interest, developed by attentive education, the orchestra has been brought to a higher and higher level by its conductors. Descended from the French bandmasters of the 17th and 18th centuries, through Weber, Mendelssohn, Berlioz, Wagner and Liszt, those great composer-conductors who established the fundamentals of orchestral performance as inherent in the correct execution of dynamics and color, the conductor now developed his own activity to the point of specialization. Conducting became a branch of the performing art just as much as the activity of an instrumental virtuoso.

Leadership in this art fell at first to Germany. Hans von Bülow (1830-1894), a pupil of Liszt and Wagner, became the first German conductor of universal importance—the man who fulfilled the ideals of Weber, Mendelssohn, Berlioz, Wagner, and Liszt. The conductor, as Bülow saw him, was to be the interpreter of the work, the technical director of the performance, and the representative of the composer. Thus he was the spiritual centre from which all the separate parts of the performance took their direction. The fulfillment of this task supposed a person combining in himself absolute authority over the orchestra with the ability to subordinate himself to the composer, demanded both artistic and moral integrity.

Subsequent development has shown that these two qualities have not always been kept in equilibrium. Some conductors incline towards virtuoso effects, some are arbitrary in the use of their power, some feel their free artistic action restricted by their moral responsibility. But apart from these natural individual differences, the type itself of the conductor has become that of the representative musician, who dominates to-day as the singing virtuoso did in the 17th and 18th centuries, and the instrumental virtuoso in his time. This fact confirms the idea of the orchestra as a unified instrument with the conductor as its player.

While leadership among conductors started from the German school, other nationalities have shared in it, though in strikingly limited number. The performances in Paris of Beethoven's symphonies under the Alsatian Habeneck (1781-1849) were studied and praised by Mendelssohn and Wagner; the most important French conductor around 1900 was Édouard Colonne (1838-1910), famous as a Berlioz specialist; well-known English conductors are Sir Henry Wood (1866-), and Sir Thomas Beecham (1879-).

THE MECHANISTIC ORCHESTRA

Italy and France have continued to produce good conductors, but the compass of their activity has been limited. In Italy concerts have always remained secondary to opera and opera itself was cultivated in only a conventional form calling for no special orchestral leadership.

Each of the most important conductors proves to have been rooted in the art of a single composer, whom he served as special interpreter. Wagner himself had educated a rather large group of conductors for his work, including Mottl (1856-1911), Seidl (1850-1898), Richter (1843-1916). Weingartner (1863-), facile rather than deep, and famous for a time as an interpreter of Berlioz and Liszt, has really been an imitator of Bülow; Nikisch (1855-1922) grew famous through his performances of Tschaikovsky and Bruckner; the particular sensibilities of Bruno Walter (1876-) have sprung from Mahler's art. Strauss has been the unsurpassed interpreter of his own works, giving them a transparency and lightness of sound and an unpretentious simplicity which no other conductor could ever reach. There have been many others, men like Mengelberg (1871-), for instance, primarily a technical educator, or Furtwaengler (1886-) whose original musical sincerity has given way to what is really superficial virtuosity.

Only two conductors have continued on Bülow's level: Gustav Mahler (1860-1911) and Arturo Toscanini (1867-). Mahler, opera and concert conductor and a dictator in both, achieved the greatest examples since the days of Bülow of the spiritual unity of stage and music, and before he died had created unforgettable models of opera performances. Toscanini, more specifically a musician than the spiritually and intellectually broader Mahler, has fulfilled the ideal of the most objective and simultaneously the most intensive performance. He has proved that the only true interpretation is to follow the composer's instructions. Toscanini's ideal—contrary to Mahler, who like Wagner, Strauss, and Mottl often arranged the works they performed—is that of the conductor as the obedient mouthpiece of the composer, nothing else. Apparently the simplest, this is in reality the most difficult of tasks, because it demands the high ability of recreation.

2

STRANGE as it may seem, the line of great conductors has not been continued since Toscanini, and he himself has never in his programs crossed the boundary occupied by contemporary art-for-art's-sake composers like Strauss, Debussy, and Puccini. He has neglected the younger generation musicians. Obviously this lack of successors and this stopping of the last great conductor at a certain point in musical development cannot be explained by accident or individual peculiarities. There must be a connection between the interpreters and their subjects. The con-

THE MECHANISTIC ORCHESTRA

ductors were the result of a great period of orchestral creation. When the force of this creation diminished, at least in that form which called for the customary type of leader, then conductors might continue to carry on this sort of work, superficially at least, for a certain period, but the creative impulse for further development along those lines was lacking.

The type of the conducting virtuoso, then, declined for the same reasons that had brought the disappearance of the earlier types of representative musician, such as the virtuoso singer and instrumentalist. This does not mean that there were no more conductors. There were and are conductors as there have continued to be singers, pianists, violinists, and other instrumentalists. But what was lacking was the production of new individualities with new intentions, new directions, new representative importance. These could grow only out of a flourishing, incessantly renewed creativity, which existed, indeed, but which sought other outlets than that of the orchestra as it had hitherto existed. The type of orchestra, the type of conductors were bound by degrees to change, because the system of musical creation itself was changing.

Looking back to the origin and progress of the modern orchestra, we recognize three principles which have determined its development since the period of the late Renaissance or about 1600. The first was the augmentation of hitherto soloistic instrumental voices to a choir or chorus. The second was the doubling of single important tones, such as the fifth or octave. The third was the basing of the instrumental body—in which these augmented voices and doubled tones made themselves manifest—upon the stringed instruments as a nucleus.

The first principle—the augmentation of the number of the instruments for the purpose of an ensemble—became the starting-point for dynamic effects. The second principle—the completion of harmony by the doubling of certain important tones—destroyed the former polyphonic style and became the starting-point for coloristic effects, because the doubling of certain tones effected a change in tone-color. Finally, the construction of the orchestra upon the string nucleus confirmed the unchangeably harmonic character of the phenomenon of orchestra. This harmonic character might, indeed, be varied, the centre of gravity could be shifted occasionally from the strings to the wood-winds or even to the brasses, but such changes were only variations of color-accent and did not affect the choral type of orchestral ensemble originating from the strings.

Now the new development following the age of art-for-art's-sake turned away from these three great principles of orchestral construction. The choral augmentation of voices in a horizontal direction that gave rise to a dynamic ensemble gave way to an opposite tendency, namely that of reduction to a soloistic group. The doubling of voices in a vertical direction, which had thrown open the whole field of coloristic development, also gave way to an opposite tendency, namely that of the earlier polyphonic emphasizing of the individual, unmixed color-value of each single instrument. And, finally, the strings—always the nucleus, more or less accentuated, of the orchestral ensemble—no longer appeared even as a family group. This group was now split up into its single parts which were employed only as individuals, as the wind instruments had been employed early in orchestral development.

This process of abolition of its choirs shows that the orchestra was no longer considered as an ensemble for the display of instrumental dynamics and color. Only the framework of this ensemble remained intact. But it was the framework no longer of an orchestral but of a chamber-music ensemble. We have already seen similar tendencies in the preceding period, especially in Brahms; but Brahms's music showed only certain restrictions of instrumental color-values in favor of a stronger emphasis on the linear features of harmony. The tendency of the new orchestral style went further. In attacking the dynamic and coloristic choral character of the orchestra, it attacked simultaneously the fundamental principle of harmony itself, the creative foundation from which orchestra had developed and to which it had held through the stylistic changes of several centuries. Now this idea of a collective unity in the orchestra as symbolic sound-medium was replaced by a separation into single more or less small groups of instruments and—consequently—of audiences.

From the hitherto prevalent point of view this change was a symptom of decay. But considering the aimlessness and the inbreeding that inevitably accompanied art created for art's sake, it signified a desire for regeneration, an examination into the true purposes of all media, an honest comparison of the organic, artistic, and social content of music. It was an experiment in revision, once again an acknowledgment of the cultural task of music and the inner justification of its forms.

3

THERE were two composers who undertook this experiment: the Austrian Arnold Schoenberg (1874-) and the Russian Igor Stravinsky (1882-). Schoenberg descended from Wagner, and his first compositions represented the logical continuation of Wagner's work. The "Gurrelieder," a great work for soloists, chorus, and orchestra, employs the large Wagner orchestra even with some additions. Likewise two one-act operas, *Die glückliche Hand* and *Erwartung* continue in the same direction, their plots reflecting Wagnerian thoughts, their musical construction also being developed from the Wagnerian resolution—that impulse toward deliverance which, as we have seen, translated from metaphysical into musical terms

THE MECHANISTIC ORCHESTRA

means the solution of harmonic action through the cadence into the final key, as in Wagner's works.

Little by little, the critical mind of Schoenberg submitted this process to a thorough examination. The result was first the stripping away of all apparently superfluous voices whose purpose had been only to fill and to enhance the harmonic dynamics and colors. As his inexorable intellect continued this method of cleaning and clearing, the big orchestra shrank to small dimensions, a new type of chamber music was discovered, first with certain relations to the old forms of the quartet, by degrees in new combinations, as the cast of *Pierrot Lunaire* shows: violin, viola, flute, piccolo, clarinet, bass-clarinet, and piano, combined with a speaking voice, marked in notes that are hinted at rather than openly declared—a voice which apparently sounds from far within and does not take on sufficient body for full musical realization. Besides making these reductions, Schoenberg in the "Orchesterstücke" op. 16 examined the instrumental colors for their special values. These pieces are written for a large orchestra and their instrumentation seems strange enough—as when in the last measures of No. 4, the muted double-basses play tremolo the chord f-a-flat-c-e in tenor, while five stopped horns blow g-b in pp. Elsewhere in this score Schoenberg's instructions are that "the change of chords must be made so softly that the newly entering instruments may be noticed only by the change in color."

As one can see, Schoenberg advances step by step. He is a revolutionary not on principle but by necessity; all he wants is to leave in existence nothing which is not absolutely essential. This tendency must lead inevitably towards the fundamental problem of the phenomenon of harmony. The romantic manifestation now appears as no definitive but only a temporary phase. Its natural progress had been halted by the same conventional crystallizations that were revealed as merely consequences of a certain stage of harmonic development. One of these crystallizations was, for instance, the idea of the keynote. Now the question arose: is the keynote with all its consequences of cadence and resolution in reality the foundation from which the scales must be built in certain steps? Or can the keynote be conceived as a centre around which all available tones may be grouped, supposing a certain lawful order is kept? Schoenberg answers the first question in the negative, the second in the affirmative, and in this way he discovers his twelve-tone scale, representing no longer a vertical but a circular order of tones.

The instruments accordingly could no longer be arranged on the basis of sounding together vertically, but must be employed in accordance with their logical relations to the centre. Their vertical simultaneity sounding together is no longer the prime purpose but an accidental consequence of the progress of the voices and must—as in the former polyphony—be

THE MECHANISTIC ORCHESTRA

taken as such. Herewith the principle of dynamics loses the creative importance it had maintained since Beethoven. A new logic, based upon the movement of the single voices, is discovered and a new rationalism of musical structure replaces the old emotional principle of development along the line of dynamic feeling.

The color-values of the instruments gain new importance. They are no longer reflections and culminations of dynamic harmonic development. They seem to be separate and independent manifestations of special moods without tendency to amalgamate, each the clear expression of a transcendental moment. The principle of thematic development is kept, but it loses its minuteness of detail. It is abbreviated, often to almost aphoristic hints; the whole creative process is constantly being refined away into clever brain-work. The instruments seem merely to trace out some sort of graspable indications in an abstract and spiritualistic world of tonal apparitions that exist only in the essence of the real sounds.

It is thin air which Schoenberg breathes, of a purely speculative region in which music becomes incorporeal and the instruments change from performing organs into signposts. Hence the process of Schoenberg's development shows an increasing estrangement from the world, from reality, even an increasing negation of those institutions which still represent the actual fullness of hitherto accepted forms. There is no longer an orchestra, only voices and some separate instruments. Even if Schoenberg goes back to old models and transcribes a concerto grosso of Handel, the effect is of the dissolving of each compact orchestral sound into tremulous hints and indications that suggest rather than convey any tonal body.

Schoenberg's work as a whole says: orchestra is finished. Likewise the process of harmonic development by dynamics and color, as it determined the music of the last centuries, is finished. A new kernel must be discovered around which a new organism may grow up, founded upon purely musical laws of construction.

Alban Berg, Schoenberg's pupil, has achieved in his operas, *Wozzeck* and the not yet performed *Lulu*, the practical application of Schoenberg's theories. Here indeed orchestra regains its former grandeur, and the result seems to contradict Schoenberg's own results, though Berg's opera construction is exactly based upon Schoenberg's principles. These operas, indeed, seem like new editions of Wagner's orchestral method, transported, it is true, into another sphere and dealing with harmony no longer as a cosmic but as an absolutely subjective, a mystic phenomenon of the soul. They present a purely polyphonic organism built of manifold thematic elements developed without regard to harmonic effect and frequently cutting across each other in sharp dissonances.

Opera here proves once more its fruitful influence upon instrumental art. One may perhaps discover a contradiction between this mighty orchestra with its moving, colorful dynamics and its singular, extraordinary, so to speak "surreal" contents, expressive of a region of subconsciousness far from even psychological reality. But only the use Berg makes of it is new. The principle itself originates in Wagner and represents, like Schoenberg's art, a final consequence of the creative stimuli of harmony. The number of the instruments, the size of this harmonic orchestra, is without significance, only its effect as a unit is important, and this has a spirit of reckless veracity, unrestrained by convention, whether of musical or of intellectual origin.

The fact is remarkable that this particular kind of music, apparently so set apart, has had, combined with the impressive action of *Wozzeck*, a far-reaching success, one of the very few successes to be registered in the decades after *Rosenkavalier*. It has thus proved its capacity and its right to exist in the practice of musical life and can no longer be set aside as only a sort of mental speculation.

4

SCHOENBERG himself, whose creative nature has to a large extent been active in his stirring abilities as a teacher, has gradually lost his influence and has steadily withdrawn from public contacts—a withdrawal that corresponds to his desertion of the orchestra. The most influential composer of the last decade, both with audiences and with young musicians, has been the Russian Igor Stravinsky. Stravinsky's musicianship rests not on harmony, not on melody or singing, not on polyphony. All these are to be found in his music, and his changing treatment of them characterizes the different stages of his work. But the fundamental element of his art is rhythm. All the various manifestations of his development are nothing but steps in the development of his primal rhythmic force.

Stravinsky starts with the dance, the Russian ballet. This includes not only conventional and unconventional dances but also pantomime with complicated action. Here language seemed to be too heavy and material and the dance opened an avenue free from its restrictions. Thus it became possible to perform ideal actions, comparable to those of symphonies, only by music and the changing picture; they were actions not of harmony, but of rhythm.

This was the principle to which Stravinsky clung even when he no longer wrote ballets. His first great works, by which he became famous, were indeed ballets, *Petrouchka*, *L'oiseau de feu*, *Le sacre du printemps*. With time he changed to pantomime like *L'histoire du soldat*, and subsequently he came to include a certain amount of language, as in *Mavra*, *Les noces*, *Oedipus rex*, *Symphonie des psaumes*, *Per-*

THE MECHANISTIC ORCHESTRA

séphone. None of these works, with exception of *Mavra*, is an opera, several of them are written characteristically to Latin texts, the construction varies. Stravinsky wrote a considerable number of purely instrumental works during the same period. One feature remains common to them all and that is the central importance of rhythm in all Stravinsky's creations.

In putting this rhythmic element to the fore and subordinating all other factors, harmony as well as melody, to the rhythmic conception, Stravinsky was obliged to alter the special means of harmonic expression, thus arriving from another starting-point than Schoenberg at the same or similar results. Dynamics, color, the means offered by the great orchestra, the type of melodic form, of constructive development —in short, all elements of the harmonic art, hitherto considered expressive, were cancelled or put aside. The dynamically colored orchestra, the orchestra centering around the strings which were in turn surrounded and illumined by the rainbow of the winds—this whole apparatus proved superfluous, even to be a hindrance, and was doomed to disappear. In its stead a new organism, a rhythmic orchestra, had to be constructed and developed.

This happened not all at once. In the beginning Stravinsky showed himself the ingenious pupil of his master Rimsky-Korsakoff. He passed through a development similar to that of Schoenberg, his large orchestra only by degrees melted away. In *L'histoire du soldat* only seven instruments are left: violin, clarinet, bassoon, cornet, trombone, double-bass, battery; in the next instrumental works the strings disappear altogether and only winds and piano remain; afterwards separate groups of strings return, *Apollon Musagéte* being scored for strings alone and the *symphonie des Psaumes* calling for flutes, oboes, trumpets, horns, piano, cello, and double-basses. The casts constantly change, but one point remains the same: the removal of the strings from their leading position as base-line of orchestra.

The introduction of *Le sacre du printemps*, a relatively early work first performed in 1913, gives an especially interesting example of this. The first part illustrates the "Fertility of the Earth" and the introduction, painting the awakening of the mystic powers of creation, may in a way—as its counterpart —be compared to Wagner's *Rheingold* prelude. Stravinsky's introduction is based upon a bassoon-solo, horns and clarinets approach with some prolonged phrases, in time the English horn and other winds are added, all of them with individualized thematic phrases. But the strings have nearly nothing to say. Some pizzicati are inserted, a trill of the violins, some rhythmic beats of the cello, a sustained tone of the double-basses, but as the winds develop an increasingly animated picture, the strings remain only as accompaniment.

THE MECHANISTIC ORCHESTRA

This picture is important as an original artistic invention. But the fact is also important that Stravinsky builds it almost without strings. He has no use for them, they are a choir and choirs hinder the unfolding of the individual voices. The strings want to sing, to give expression, and that is what Stravinsky does not want. His orchestra is a rhythmic organism. The rhythms themselves change incessantly, often from measure to measure. They not only change in succession, they are also combined simultaneously in various ways.

This was not a new thing. Mozart had already combined three different rhythms in the famous minuet from *Don Giovanni*, when 3/4, 2/4, and 3/8 occur together. But this was an exception, made legitimate by the different types of aristocratic and peasant dances. Stravinsky's polyrhythm is the manifestation of his dependence upon a rhythmic foundation, of his avoidance of dynamics. It is in principle the same as Strauss, Debussy, or Puccini writing different dynamics in perhaps three levels simultaneously.

In Stravinsky's scores the dynamic instructions are limited to very few and these quite general. There is no longer a crescendo or a decrescendo, there are no different degrees of piano or of forte, if such marks appear at all. The orchestra tends to be mechanical, acrobatic, and its main aim is to express not changing feelings but solid objectivity, not emotion but motion. It is a visual conception of music. Its ideal model is no longer the singer but the dancer. Therefore instruments of the singing type, the strings, must be eliminated or at least their singing qualities cut out. All principles of doubling and coloring must be changed. The idea of rhythm as the creative impulse of music is proclaimed as the new law of form construction and of orchestra.

5

THE replacement of the expressive power of music by its motor power, the supersession of the poetic dynamism by the static structural principle, the change from inner feeling as the leading constructive force to external gesture; this was quite a new conception of music. But perhaps not wholly new, for the first half of the 18th century had worked along similar principles and only the development from Beethoven toward romanticism had put them in secondary place.

Now the exhaustion of the purely dynamic stimulus brought about a reassembling of these former principles and at the same time a renewed turning towards the art of composers of the pre-Beethoven period—Bach, Handel, Pergolese, and others. In a new aesthetics, Busoni rediscovered music as a game of moving tones, from which poetic, philosophic, spiritual elements in general—the natural symptoms of the dynamic impulse—were eliminated. The mo-

THE MECHANISTIC ORCHESTRA

tor power in tonal relations and weights became the directing force.

This change was caused not alone by exhaustion of and disgust for the dynamic principles. It paralleled similar impulses in other fields. Technical inventions, the film and radio in particular, had revealed the fruitfulness of motor force as a stimulant. Both radio and film were first utilized as new media in opera by Pfitzner, Berg, and Krenek, and Respighi had even employed the gramophone record as an instrument for imitating the voice of the nightingale. But the unchaining of these newly recognized elements went further in its effect and furnished a new aim for creative activity. Stravinsky was able to gain such wide influence mainly because of the general circumstances: on the one hand the exhaustion of the dynamic impulse, on the other, the new awareness of the creative force of motor power.

In this connection the new type of dance orchestra should not be overlooked. It came from America and was the first original American contribution to the orchestral and thus to the musical affairs of Europe. The most characteristic mark of this dance orchestra was the disappearance of the strings and their replacement by those wood-winds which had hitherto been looked upon as bastards, unworthy of admission to the symphonic orchestra: the family of the saxophones. With them appeared a new group of provocative percussion-instruments of different types.

All these together, united in a small group, represented a new type of the dance itself, its rhythms, its climaxes, its forms.

So far as concerns rhythm, it was an exotic element, derived from negro music, which thus penetrated into European music. But these apparently foreign elements revealed themselves on closer observation as variations, distortions, transformations of Western prototypes which had been altered by new climatic and spiritual influences. This new type of dances and dance music opened a new field for instrumental activity no less or more important and stimulating than the pavane of the 17th, the gavotte and the minuet of the 18th, the valse of the 19th centuries. The young composers in every country participated in this new activity. The post-war generation strove to rid music of the ponderous intellectual attributes of the pre-war period. Return to music itself, without philosophical, aesthetic, or ethical burden, became the watchword and this watchword was identifiable with the result of Schoenberg's and Stravinsky's development. It became authoritative in France for the so-called "Six," among whom Milhaud, Poulenc and the Swiss Honegger—all leaning upon that singular older person Eric Satie (1866-1925)—were prominent in claiming a new archaic style. Similar groups of young revolutionary talents stirred in England, in Austria and Germany, and in America, which last and timidly, but with quickly

THE MECHANISTIC ORCHESTRA

growing interest, now entered the West-European music circle.

The most remarkable among these young composers who followed the new direction was Paul Hindemith. He continued the principle of Stravinsky's work, transporting it into a purely musical sphere, freed from all relation with, even from any reminiscence of the dance. In Hindemith's compositions the merely instrumental—one might say the symphonic—instinct again gains the upper hand; even in his operas the voices and the action are subordinate to the play of motor power. Laws of formal construction dominate, all expressive elements must go. The tendency to structural development supersedes all dynamic and coloristic interests, and that quality which has been called "kinetic energy" proves to be the ruling principle.

But what of orchestra in the face of such conditions?

The hitherto fundamental principle of an orchestra in which all details are exactly disposed, begins to weaken. In his cantata "Der Plöner Musiktag," Hindemith calls for an instrumental cast in which, however, each single instrument may be changed if necessary and replaced by another. This is a special case, but it characterizes the fundamental idea. It means a return to the method of the 17th and 18th centuries, where those instruments were used which were at hand and the essence of the work was independent of special instrumental color. The instrument had to play a voice—that was its main task, and the conception of the work did not assume a performance dependent upon the special qualities of the instruments. With this move, the hitherto acknowledged principles of orchestra seemed to be cancelled, especially as creative production in Europe showed a steady decline.

It may perhaps be said that such countries as England and especially America, which came last to participate in orchestral development, have not only created the best orchestras of the present time but also show a constantly increasing interest in the cultivation of orchestral forms, so that one might think the centre of gravity of production had shifted from East to West. But again, the likewise increased musical activity in Russia should not be overlooked. The imitation of traditional West-European forms and figures, moreover, temporarily still dominates both in America and in Russia. The task remains to accommodate these European forms to the changed sociological conditions of the West, supposing that orchestral forms show sufficient elasticity for such organic change.

The present picture gives no clue to whether or not this task is being carried out. The orchestras in America as well as in Europe make up their programs mainly from works of former periods. The audiences like to hear mostly these works, which give them an

THE MECHANISTIC ORCHESTRA

illusion of the past. New works appear seldom and without success. No composer since Stravinsky has found general recognition and even Stravinsky's success has been fading. His most-performed works were originally written not as concert works but for the stage; they are suites composed for ballets. His other works mostly belong to the field of chamber music, like those of the German Hindemith, the Frenchman Milhaud, the Italians Casella and Malipiero. The older French master Ravel (1875-) is certainly a dexterous craftsman, but neither a penetrating nor a convincing innovator, and remains confined to the pre-war limits of his art, as does also—despite his remarkable harmonic peculiarities—the German Brahms-successor, Max Reger. The Russian Scriabine has tried to discover a new orchestral climax by combining musical with actual color-effects, performed by a special apparatus. There are experiments enough, but true and effective symphonic production has become very rare, and a new type of form and sonority, based upon the orchestra in its hitherto known construction, is wholly lacking.

6

FROM the orchestral stage it would seem that music itself now lives only on its heritage. Contemporary production in other fields of music also, in opera, in chamber music, in songs, can hardly achieve general recognition and is supported mainly by small circles of connoisseurs. The public effect is always the same: an unconcealed resistance of the audiences to new productions, a demonstrative favoritism toward earlier works. This seems the more remarkable if we remember that the periods of Bach, Handel, Haydn, Mozart, Beethoven, or even those of Palestrina and older masters, show just the contrary picture, namely a constant need for new works and an only occasional desire to revive old works.

Our orchestral concerts exhibit this picture in an especially striking light. They are established on an economic basis, but the artistic impetus is lacking. These concerts consist only of repetitions, repetitions of good works, indeed, but with only a historical relation to the present and with no view to the future. They are merely museum affairs. They live on the interest from a great capital, but they do not augment that capital. The works they perform will keep alive as long and as far as their innate strength extends. To perpetuate them will remain a task of orchestras, whether they play in concert halls or for the records or on the radio. This is a permanent factor in the education of the people and for this purpose orchestras will have to continue to exist.

But the motive underlying the creation of orchestral music, the force that has ruled it for more than 200 years—can they longer be continued?

The orchestra has only been a medium for the exposition of harmonic forces, and all forms of orches-

THE MECHANISTIC ORCHESTRA

tral music were to be explained as growing up from the one common root: harmony. Yet these forms were incessantly changing. Why were they so different?

The reason cannot be discovered exclusively in musical conditions. Music does not change by itself. Experience proves that people of all times have favored the existing forms of music. There have always been difficulties, controversies, fights about new forms, in earlier times as well as in the days of Mozart and Beethoven, of Berlioz and Wagner, of Stravinsky and Schoenberg. Nevertheless the new forms have always maintained themselves successfully with time, because the causes which made them grow up have proved stronger than the resistance against them.

This resistance arose from the habit of thought which tends to hold as permanent the laws that have hitherto controlled production while the new period has established its own laws beyond argument. But the reasons which enforced the changes originated in the most powerful of all elements of human communal existence: in the elementary conditions of social life. The story of the orchestra is one of the most significant records of these conditions.

The story of the orchestra shows from its beginning an overwhelming abundance of great figures. They first appear in the period of the Renaissance. They pass to the thorough-bass period in the first half of the 18th century. They continue to the classic period of Haydn, Mozart, Beethoven, thence to Schubert, Mendelssohn, Berlioz, Liszt, Wagner, Brahms, Bruckner, Strauss, Debussy, Stravinsky. The history of their works is indeed a history of the combining of many instruments on changing principles; it is a story of changing forms, varied by the individualities of ingenious musicians, and, finally, it is the record of the unfolding of harmony, which includes by its physical nature the driving principles of expansion and contraction.

Yet all these aspects cover but partial manifestations of the one and only fundamental force: social change. All arts are moved and changed by this social force. Music especially exists as a social phenomenon, throwing an invisible thread from one individual to another unknown individual, binding them together, attracting an ever-increasing number and forming in this way a new collective organism.

This social force constitutes the true creative impulse behind all changes in the orchestra. A bird's eye view of the story of the orchestra shows us the story of the changing social relations and changing communal interests of men.

We may regard these relations from points of view which give them political significance. Then we find their starting-point in the gradual loosening of mediaeval collectivism. We pass through the patriarchal thorough-bass epoch to the liberation of the individ-

THE MECHANISTIC ORCHESTRA

ual by the democratic community of the classic orchestra, the most perfect manifestation of rational balance and the equal rights of all forces. This culminates in the growing autocracy of the single individual in the 19th century, and finishes with the decay of this exaggerated individualism and the present reversion to the opposite extreme of a new collectivism. We may regard this process from the standpoint of intellectual interests. Then we observe the struggle between the idea of reason, which arises during the 17th and dominates the 18th century, and the gradual spread of emotion, with its dissolving and obscuring influence, during the 19th century. We may regard this same process from the physical point of view, as the ascendancy of mechanization.

But in the last analysis it is not any of these political, intellectual, or physical aspects alone that govern the growth of our art. It is the influence of human society itself, incessantly changing and growing.

We see in the beginning the amateurs of music, meeting for the performance of an opera or a concert, arranged for bringing people together. We see how this circle enlarged with the increasing importance of its purpose. As the other common meeting places, especially the church, lost their unifying force, the concert gained more and more power of attraction. It became the place where the dominating ideas, the moving impulses of the new time, were proclaimed and where they came to full expression.

THE STORY OF THE ORCHESTRA

At this point the history of the present day orchestra really begins. This orchestra became the representative of a new class of listeners, of a new audience, unacquainted until then with music, drawn to it not by fancy or desire for entertainment, but by spiritual necessity. We see that with time this circle grew steadily and that the task of the orchestra also enlarged steadily, the disposition of its mechanism as well as the organization of its forms also having to be enlarged. In this sense, it was not the music and it was not the creative musician—it was the audience, which wrote the story of the orchestra.

And vice versa, this story of the orchestra is the story of its audiences. There was no other instrument, no other form-organization which could be compared to the orchestra as an organism for the reproduction of common thoughts, common feelings, common tendencies and aims. No other form-organization reflected all these movements as directly as the orchestra, because its entity was founded upon the human community and because its laws were directed by each movement of this community. For this reason orchestra has been and will still continue to be one of the most important phenomena of human culture.

Index

Amati, Andrea (1530-1611), 19
Atterberg (1887-), 254
Auber (1782-1871), 144

Bach, Joh. Seb. (1685-1750), 30, 33, 36, 39, 41, 45, 47, 51, 100, 101, 205, 209, 222, 256, 261, 306, 312
Bach, Philip Emanuel (1714-1788), 42, 51, 52, 54, 55, 57, 59
Balakireff (1837-1910), 248, 249
Banister (1630-1679), 33
Bantock (1868-), 254
Bartók (1881-), 254
Beecham (1879-), 288
Beethoven (1770-1827), 29, 39, 40, 46, 50, 61, 74, 87, 88-107, 118, 120, 121, 122, 124, 128, 130, 132, 138, 140, 145, 146, 149, 155, 156, 168, 169, 173, 174, 176, 194, 198, 199, 200, 201, 202, 203, 205, 209, 210, 211, 212, 213, 214, 215, 216, 217, 218, 219, 220, 224, 226, 232, 244, 256-262, 263, 265, 288, 299, 306, 312, 313, 314
Bellini (1801-1835), 236, 256, 278
Berg (1885-1936), 300-301, 307
Berlioz (1803-1869), 89, 137, 142-158, 159, 162, 165, 166, 168, 169, 173, 174, 176, 183, 187, 193, 199, 200, 201, 202, 225, 226, 228, 233, 234, 240, 248, 250, 256, 264, 265, 272, 287, 283, 313, 314
Bizet (1838-1875), 228, 240-243, 256

Borodin (1834-1887), 248
Brahms (1833-1897), 143, 201, 203-227, 228, 245, 253, 256, 295, 314
Britton (1651-1678), 33
Bruckner (1824-1896), 201, 203, 216-227, 228, 249, 256, 272, 314
Bülow, Hans von (1830-1894), 170, 211, 287, 290
Busoni (1866-1924), 306

Cannabich (1731-1798), 57
Casella (1883-), 311
Catherine the Great (1729-1796), 246
Catherine de Medici (1519-1589), 28
Cherubini (1760-1842), 128, 142, 143, 256
Chopin (1810-1849), 148, 159, 162, 167
Cimarosa (1749-1801), 246
Colonne (1838-1910), 288
Corelli (1653-1713), 36
Couperin, François (le Grand) (1668-1733), 276

Debussy (1862-1818), 256, 263, 264, 271-278, 279, 282, 290, 305, 314
Delius (1863-1934), 254
Dohnányi (1877-), 254
Donizetti (1797-1848), 236, 278
Durante (1684-1755), 52
Dvořak (1841-1904), 245

Elgar (1857-1934), 228, 254, 256

(317)

INDEX

Elizabeth (Queen) (1533-1603), 28
Esterhazy, Prince, 42, 45, 46, 48, 63

Franck (1822-1890), 272, 273
Frederick the Great (1712-1786), 55
Frescobaldi (1583-1643), 34
Furtwängler (1886-), 289

Gabrieli, Andrea (1510-1586), 34, 35
Gabrieli, Giovanni (1557-1612), 34, 35
Gade (1817-1890), 254
Garcia, Manuel (1805-1906), 148
Garcia, Maria (Mme. Malibran) (1808-1836), 148
Garcia, Pauline (Mme. Viardot) (1821-1910), 148
Gaviniès (1726-1800), 52
Gellert (1715-1769), 39
Glasunoff (1865-), 248
Glinka (1804-1857), 247
Gluck (1714-1787), 39, 46, 75, 78, 84, 85, 128, 142, 143, 174, 256, 260
Goethe (1749-1832), 224
Gossec (1734-1829), 58
Gounod (1818-1893), 256
Graziani (1605-1664), 30
Grétry (1742-1813), 73, 76, 142, 195, 256
Grieg (1843-1907), 254

Habeneck (1781-1849), 140, 288
Handel (1685-1759), 29, 30, 33, 34, 39, 41, 46, 67, 78, 90, 100, 173, 222, 256, 300, 306, 312
Hasse (1699-1783), 78
Haydn (1732-1809), 16, 39-67, 73, 78, 79, 80, 87, 88, 90, 93, 94, 95, 100, 101, 102, 103, 105, 106, 110, 112, 115, 138, 145, 169, 173, 174, 194, 201, 202, 224, 244, 256, 312, 314
Heckel, 266
Henry VIII (1491-1547), 28
Herder (1744-1803), 40

Hindemith (1895-), 309, 311
Honegger (1892-), 308
Hubay (1858-), 254
Hugo (1802-1885), 168
Hume (1711-1776), 40

d'Indy (1851-1927), 272

Janacek (1854-1918), 245

Kant (1724-1804), 40
King (about 1690), 33
Kodály (1882-), 254
Krenek (1900-), 307

Lablache (1794-1858), 148
Lamartine (1790-1869), 168
Le Gros, 46
Lessing (1729-1781), 39
Lesueur (1760-1837), 145
Liszt (1811-1886), 148, 155, 156, 162-172, 173, 174, 176, 183, 193, 199, 200, 201, 202, 204, 206, 228, 233, 248, 256, 264, 287, 314
Lobkowitz, Prince, 91
Louis XIV (1638-1715), 69, 74
Löwe (1865-1925), 221
Lully (1632-1682), 54, 69-74, 78, 139, 142, 143, 173, 174, 256, 260

Maelzel (1772-1838) (inventor of the metronome), 97
Maeterlinck (1862-), 275
Mahler (1860-1911), 201, 203, 222-227, 228, 256, 289, 290
Malipiero (1882-), 311
Mannheim composers, 54, 58, 59
Martinu, 246
Mehul (1763-1817), 142
Mendelssohn (1809-1847), 118-121, 133-137, 139-141, 142, 143, 146, 170, 173, 200, 201, 202, 204, 226, 256, 287, 288, 314
Mengelberg (1871-), 289
Meyerbeer (1791-1864), 144-145, 146, 157-165, 166, 167, 171, 173, 193, 201, 202, 228, 234, 238, 240, 256, 264

(318)

INDEX

Milhaud (1892-), 308, 311
Monteverdi (1567-1643), 28, 30, 39, 67-70, 78, 256, 268
Morzin, Count, 42, 48
Mottl (1856-1911), 289
Mozart (1756-1791), 16, 45, 51, 64, 75, 78-87, 88, 93, 94, 100, 102, 103, 105, 108, 112, 116, 173, 174, 198, 232, 244, 256, 257, 259, 260, 266, 281, 305, 312, 313, 314
Mussorgsky (1839-1881), 247, 248, 256, 274
Mustel (1840-1893), 266

Nielsen (1865-), 254
Nikisch (1855-1922), 289

Paganini (1782-1840), 148, 149, 155
Palestrina (1526-1594), 312
Pergolese (1710-1736), 52, 306
Pfitzer (1869-), 307
Philidor (1726-1795), 33
Porpora (1686-1766), 42
Poulenc (1899-), 308
Praetorius (1571-1621), 22
Puccini (1858-1924), 256, 263, 264, 278-283, 290, 305
Purcell (1658-1695), 256

Rameau (1683-1764), 39, 74, 78, 142, 173, 222, 260
Ravel (1875-), 311
Reger (1873-1916), 256, 311
Rembrandt (1606-1669), 101
Respighi (1879-1936), 307
Richter, Franz Xavier (1709-1789), 57
Richter, Hans (1843-1916), 289
Rimsky-Korsakoff (1844-1908), 247, 248, 303
Rossini (1792-1868), 143, 234-236, 256
Rousseau (1712-1778), 40
Rubini (1795-1854), 148
Rückert (1788-1866), 224

Sachs (1881-), xi
Salo, Gasparo da (1542-1609) 19

Satie (1866-1925), 308
Sax (1814-1894), inventor of the saxophone, 234
Scarlatti, Alessandro (1659-1725), 54, 70-71, 78
Scarlatti, Domenico (1685-1757), 52
Schalk (1863-1930), 221
Schiller (1759-1805), 168
Schoenberg (1874), 256, 284, 296-301, 303, 308, 313
Schopenhauer (1788-1860), 181
Schreker (1878-1934), 266
Schubert (1794-1828), 118-122, 130-133, 146, 167, 174, 200, 201, 202, 223, 226, 314
Schumann (1810-1856), 120, 122, 132, 137-138, 146, 148, 173, 174, 200, 212, 226, 256, 275
Schuppanzich (1776-1830), 265
Scriabine (1872-1915), 311
Seidl (1850-1898), 289
Sibelius (1865-), 228, 254, 256
Sinding (1856-), 254
Smetana (1824-1884), 228, 243-245, 253, 256
Spohr (1784-1859) (conductor), 119, 139
Spontini (1774-1851), 143, 256, 260
Stamitz (1717-1757), 57, 256
Stradivarius (1644-1737), 19
Strauss, Richard (1864-), 150, 233, 256, 263-271, 274, 278, 279, 281, 282, 289, 290, 305, 314
Stravinsky (1882-), 256, 263, 284, 296, 301-311, 313, 314
Suk (1874-1934), 246

Taneïeff (1856-1915), 248
Tartini (1692-1770), 52
Thorwaldsen (1770-1844), 214
Tomasini (1741-1808), 48
Toscanini (1867-), 289, 290
Tschaïkovsky (1840-1893), 228, 248-253, 256

Verdi (1813-1901), 143, 228, 235-240, 241, 256, 257, 278

(319)

INDEX

Vivaldi (1680-1743), 36
Vogler, Abbé (1749-1814), 144

Wagner (1813-1883), 64, 74, 89, 135, 140, 143, 144, 156, 160, 172, 173-198, 199, 200, 201, 202, 205, 206, 210, 219, 220, 221, 223, 225, 226, 232, 233, 238, 239, 240, 242, 245, 248, 250, 253, 256, 257, 259, 260, 261, 266, 268, 273, 274, 287, 288, 290, 296, 297, 300, 303, 313, 314
Walter (1876-), 289
Weber (1786-1826), 118-129, 131, 132, 137, 139, 142, 143, 144, 146, 147, 151, 152, 155, 173, 174, 187, 188, 193, 201, 202, 204, 226, 228, 253, 256, 287
Weingartner (1863-), 289
Williams (1872-), 254
Wood (1866-), 288